DATE DUE

DEMCO 38-297

JERRY BRIDGES & THE
PRACTICE OF GODLINESS

NAVPRESS ◢
A Ministry of The Navigators
P.O. Box 6000, Colorado Springs, CO 80934

The Navigators is an international Christian organization. Jesus Christ gave His followers the Great Commission to go and make disciples (Matthew 28:19). The aim of The Navigators is to help fulfill that commission by multiplying laborers for Christ in every nation.

NavPress is the publishing ministry of The Navigators. NavPress publications are tools to help Christians grow. Although publications alone cannot make disciples or change lives, they can help believers learn biblical discipleship, and apply what they learn to their lives and ministries.

© 1983 by Jerry Bridges
All rights reserved, including translation
Library of Congress Catalog Card Number:
    83-61499
ISBN 08910-94970

Tenth printing, 1988

Unless otherwise identified, Scripture quotations are from the *Holy Bible: New International Version* (NIV). Copyright © 1973, 1978, 1984, International Bible Society. Used by permission of Zondervan Bible Publishers. Other versions used include *The King James Version* (KJV); *The Amplified New Testament* (AMP), © The Lockman Foundation 1954, 1958; *The New American Standard Bible* (NASB), © The Lockman Foundation 1960, 1962, 1963, 1968, 1971, 1972, 1973, 1975, 1977; and *The Good News Bible: The Bible in Today's English Version* (TEV), © 1976 by the American Bible Society.

Printed in the United States of America

To

My Wife

Eleanor

*God's gracious provision
of a helper suitable for me.*

Contents

Author		9
Preface		11
1	Value for All Things *1 Timothy 4:8*	15
2	Devotion to God *Revelation 15:4*	23
3	Train Yourself to Be Godly *1 Timothy 4:7*	41
4	Seeking a Deeper Devotion *Psalm 119:10*	57
5	Taking on God's Character *Colossians 3:12*	69
6	Humility *Luke 18:14*	89
7	Contentment *1 Timothy 6:6*	105
8	Thankfulness *Psalm 100:4-5*	123
9	Joy *Romans 14:17*	133
10	Holiness *1 John 1:5*	147
11	Self-Control *Proverbs 25:28*	161
12	Faithfulness *Proverbs 20:6*	177
13	Peace *Romans 12:18*	189
14	Patience *Colossians 3:12-13*	203
15	Gentleness *Galatians 5:22-23, Colossians 3:12*	219
16	Kindness and Goodness *Galatians 6:10*	231
17	Love *Colossians 3:14*	245
18	Reaching the Goal *2 Timothy 4:7*	261

Author

Jerry Bridges is Vice President for Corporate Affairs of The Navigators. He formerly served as Treasurer of The Navigators as well as in Navigator field ministries in California, Missouri, and Holland. He holds a B.S. in general engineering from the University of Oklahoma and is a former officer of the U.S. Navy.

He and his wife, Eleanor, have two adult children and live in Colorado Springs.

Jerry is also the author of *The Pursuit of Holiness*, *The Crisis of Caring* (originally published as *True Fellowship*), and *Trusting God*.

Preface

This book is a sequel to an earlier book, *The Pursuit of Holiness*. In Ephesians 4:20-24, Paul urges us to put off our old self and to put on the new self. *The Pursuit of Holiness* dealt largely with putting off the old self—dealing with sin in our lives. *The Practice of Godliness* focuses on putting on the new self—growing in Christian character.

The most well-known list of Christian character traits is the ninefold list in Galatians 5:22-23, which Paul calls the fruit of the Spirit. But there are other lists in passages such as Colossians 3:12-16, Ephesians 4:2-3 and 32, James 3:17, and 2 Peter 1:5-7 that are just as important to our understanding of what constitutes Christian character. I've incorporated most of these in this series of studies.

While in the process of doing a series of Bible studies on Christian character traits, I became interested in the subject of godliness. As my knowledge of that topic grew, I became convinced that any treatment of Christian character would be incomplete without the inclusion of a study on godliness.

Godliness is more than Christian character. It covers the totality of the Christian life and provides the foundation upon which Christian character is built. Thus the first four chapters deal with the general theme of godliness, and the remaining chapters consider important character traits of the godly person.

The order in which the studies of the various character traits appear is deliberate. The first four—humility, contentment, thankfulness, and joy—deal largely with our relationship to God. The next group of three—holiness, self-control, and faithfulness—are qualities that require us to deal sternly with ourselves. The final six—peace, patience, gentleness, kindness, goodness, and love—are qualities that enable us to deal graciously and tenderly with others. These last two divisions reflect the seeming dichotomy of Christian character: sternness with ourselves and tenderness toward others. Only the Holy Spirit can create such a beautiful diversity of sternness and tenderness within a single human personality.

The variety of topics covered in a book of this nature requires that each subject be treated only briefly. My objective is to create an awareness of the importance of each of the aspects of godliness and provide some practical suggestions for growing in them. Hopefully, many readers will be stimulated to do further study on some of the topics of particular interest to them.

As I studied the subjects of both godliness and Christian character, I was somewhat amazed that I could find so little that has been previously written on these subjects. Consequently, I have had to plow new ground in some areas. This has forced me back to the Scriptures more than if I had had the advantage of the writings of previous generations. My one qualification for presenting these studies, then, lies in thirty years of personal Bible study using methods and tools available to any layman.

There is a certain sense of anxiety in committing these studies to print which comes from the warning of James that, "Not many of you should presume to be teachers, my brothers, because you know that we who teach will be judged more strictly" (James 3:1). I am keenly aware of the need for more growth in my own life in many of the areas covered in this book. It is my prayer, however, that both author and readers will grow together as we practice godliness.

This book should be studied more than read. To facilitate that study, I have prepared a companion Bible study to be used in conjunction with this book. Though the book text is complete in itself, the use of the companion Bible study will enable the reader and student to gain a better grasp of the scriptural truths taught.

I am deeply indebted to the staff of NavPress for their encouragement to write this book and for their help in preparing the manuscript for final production.

1
Value for All Things

FOR PHYSICAL TRAINING IS OF
SOME VALUE, BUT GODLINESS HAS
VALUE FOR ALL THINGS, HOLDING
PROMISE FOR BOTH THE PRESENT
LIFE AND THE LIFE TO COME.

1 Timothy 4:8

There is no higher compliment that can be paid to a Christian than to call him a godly person. He might be a conscientious parent, a zealous church worker, a dynamic spokesman for Christ, or a talented Christian leader; but none of these things matters if, at the same time, he is not a godly person.

The words *godly* and *godliness* actually appear only a few times in the New Testament; yet the entire Bible is a book on godliness. And when those words do appear they are pregnant with meaning and instruction for us.

When Paul wants to distill the essence of the Christian life into one brief paragraph, he focuses on godliness. He tells us that God's grace "teaches us to say 'No' to *ungodliness* and worldly passions, and to

15

live self-controlled, upright and *godly* lives," as we await the coming of our Lord Jesus Christ (Titus 2:11-13). When Paul thinks of his own job description as an apostle of Jesus Christ, he describes it as being called to further the faith of God's elect and their knowledge of the truth that leads to *godliness* (Titus 1:1).

In his first letter to Timothy, Paul emphasizes godliness. We are to pray for those in authority, that we may live peaceful and quiet lives in all *godliness* and holiness. We are to train ourselves to be *godly*. We are to pursue *godliness*—the word *pursue* indicating unrelenting, persevering effort. *Godliness* with contentment is held forth as great gain; and finally, *godliness* has value for all things, holding promise for both the present life and the life to come.

When Peter, in looking forward to the day of the Lord when the earth and everything in it will be destroyed, asks what kind of people we ought to be, he answers that we are to live holy and *godly* lives (2 Peter 3:10-12). Here Peter uses the most momentous event of all history to stir us up to our Christian duty—to live holy and *godly* lives.

Surely, then, godliness is no optional spiritual luxury for a few quaint Christians of a bygone era or for some group of super-saints of today. It is both the privilege and duty of every Christian to pursue godliness, to train himself to be godly, to study diligently the practice of godliness. We don't need any special talent or equipment. God has given to each one of us "everything we need for life and godliness" (2 Peter 1:3). The most ordinary Christian has all that he needs, and the most talented Christian must use those same means in the practice of godliness.

What then is godliness? What are the marks of a godly person? How does a person become godly? I have asked a number of people the question, "What do you think of when you think of godliness?" The answers, though varied, always end up expressing some idea of Christian character, using such expression as "Godlike," "Christlike," or "the fruit of the Spirit." Godliness certainly includes Christian character, but it is more than that. There is another, even more fundamental aspect of godliness than godly character. It is the foundation, in fact, on which godly character is built.

Devotion in action

The Bible begins to give us some clues about godliness in its earliest pages. Genesis 5:21-24 tells us about Enoch, the father of Methuselah. In a very short three-verse summary of Enoch's life, Moses twice describes him as one who "walked with God." The author of Hebrews gives Enoch a place in his great "Faith's Hall of Fame" in chapter 11, but he sees Enoch from a slightly different perspective. He describes him as "one who pleased God." Here, then, are two important clues: Enoch walked with God, and Enoch pleased God. It is evident from these two statements that Enoch's life was centered in God; God was the focal point, the polestar of his very existence.

Enoch walked with God; he enjoyed a relationship with God; and he pleased God. We could accurately say he was devoted to God. This is the meaning of godliness. The New Testament word for godliness, in its original meaning, conveys the idea of a personal attitude toward God that results in actions that are pleasing to God.[1] This personal attitude toward God is what we call devotion to God. But it is always *devotion in action*. It is not just a warm, emotional feeling about God, the kind of feeling we may get while singing some grand old hymn of praise or some modern-day chorus of worship. Neither is devotion to God merely a time of private Bible reading and prayer, a practice we sometimes call "devotions." Although this practice is vitally important to a godly person, we must not think of it as defining devotion for us.

Focused on God

Devotion is not an activity; it is an attitude toward God. This attitude is composed of three essential elements:

- the fear of God
- the love of God
- the desire for God.

We will look at these elements in detail in chapter two; but for now, note that all three elements focus upon God. *The practice of godliness is an exercise or discipline that focuses upon God.* From this Godward attitude arises the character and conduct that we usually think of as godliness. So often we try to develop Christian character and conduct without taking the time to develop God-centered devotion. We try to please God without taking the time to walk with him and develop a relationship with him. This is impossible to do.

Consider the exacting requirements of a godly

lifestyle as expounded by the saintly William Law. Law uses the word *devotion* in a broader sense to mean all that is involved in godliness—actions as well as attitude:

> Devotion signifies a life given, or devoted to God. He therefore is the devout [godly] man, who lives no longer to his own will, or the way and spirit of the world, but to the sole will of God, who considers God in everything, who serves God in everything, who makes all the parts of his common life, parts of piety [godliness], by doing everything in the name of God, and under such rules as are conformable to his Glory.[2]

Note the totality of godliness over one's entire life in Law's description of the godly person. Nothing is excluded. God is at the center of his thoughts. His most ordinary duties are done with an eye to God's glory. In Paul's words to the Corinthians, whether he eats or drinks or whatever he does, he does it all for the glory of God

Now it is obvious that such a God-centered lifestyle cannot be developed and maintained apart from a solid foundation of devotion to God. Only a strong personal relationship with the living God can keep such a commitment from becoming oppressive and legalistic. John writes that God's commands are not burdensome; a godly life is not wearisome, but this is true only because a godly person is first of all devoted to God.

Devotion to God, then, is the mainspring of godly character. And this devotion is the only motivation for Christian behavior that is pleasing to God.

This motivation is what separates the godly person from the moral person, or the benevolent person, or the zealous person. The godly person is moral, benevolent, and zealous because of his devotion to God. And his life takes on a dimension that reflects the very stamp of God.

It is sad that many Christians do not have this aura of godliness about them. They may be very talented and personable, or very busy in the Lord's work, or even apparently successful in some avenues of Christian service, and still not be godly. Why? Because they are not devoted to God. They may be devoted to a vision, or to a ministry, or to their own reputation as a Christian, but not to God.

Godliness is more than Christian character: It is Christian character that springs from a devotion to God. But it is also true that devotion to God *always* results in godly character. As we study the three essential elements of devotion in the next chapter, we will see that all of them, individually and collectively, must express themselves in a life that is pleasing to God. So the definition of godliness we will use in this book is *devotion to God which results in a life that is pleasing to him.*

In the first few chapters of this book we will concentrate on this devotion, seeking to understand what it is and why it results in Christian character. In the later chapters we will look at individual traits of godly character. But we must never lose sight of the fact that devotion to God is the mainspring of Christian character and the only foundation upon which it can be successfully built.

Notes

1. Vine's *Expository Dictionary of New Testament Words* defines godliness as, "to be devout, denotes that piety which, characterized by a Godward attitude, does that which is well-pleasing to Him" (Nashville, Tenn.: Royal Publishers, n.d., page 492). J.C. Connell defines godliness as a personal attitude to God and the actions that spring directly from it (*New Bible Dictionary*, London: Inter-Varsity Fellowship, 1962, page 480).
2. William Law, *A Serious Call To a Devout and Holy Life* (Grand Rapids, Mich.: Sovereign Grace Publishers, 1971), page 1.

2
Devotion to God

WHO WILL NOT FEAR YOU, O
LORD, AND BRING GLORY TO
YOUR NAME? FOR YOU ALONE ARE
HOLY. ALL NATIONS WILL COME
AND WORSHIP BEFORE YOU, FOR
YOUR RIGHTEOUS ACTS HAVE
BEEN REVEALED.

Revelation 15:4

Enoch walked with God, and Enoch pleased God. His walk with God speaks of his relationship with God, or his devotion to God; his pleasing God speaks of the behavior that arose from that relationship. It is impossible to build a Christian behavior pattern without the foundation of a devotion to God. The practice of godliness is first of all the cultivation of a relationship with God, and from this the cultivation of a life that is pleasing to God. Our concept of God and our relationship with him determine our conduct.

We have already seen that devotion to God consists of three essential elements: the fear of God, the love of God, and the desire for God. Think of a triangle representing devotion to God, with these three elements as each of its three points.

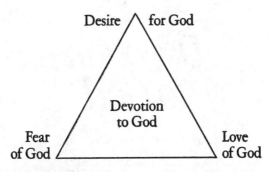

The fear of God and the love of God form the base of the triangle, while the desire for God is at the apex. As we study these elements individually, we will see that the fear of God and the love of God form the foundation of true devotion to God, while the desire for God is the highest expression of that devotion.

The God-fearing Christian

The late professor John Murray said, "The fear of God is the soul of godliness."[1] Yet the fear of God is a concept that seems old-fashioned and antiquated to many modern-day Christians. There was a time when an earnest believer might have been known as a "God-fearing man." Today we would probably be embarrassed by such language. Some seem to think the fear of God is strictly an Old Testament concept that passed away with the revelation of God's love in Christ. After all, doesn't perfect love drive out fear, as John declares in 1 John 4:18?

Although it is true that the concept of the fear of God is treated more extensively in the Old Testament, it would be a mistake to assume that it is not important in the New Testament. One of the blessings of the new covenant is the implanting in believers' hearts of the fear of the Lord. In Jeremiah 32:40 God said, "I will make an everlasting covenant with them: I will never stop doing good to them, and I will inspire them to *fear me*, so that they will never turn away from me."

"Nothing could be more significant," observed John Murray, "than that the fear of the Lord should be coupled with the comfort of the Holy Spirit as the characteristics of the New Testament church: 'So the church . . . walking in the fear of the Lord and in the comfort of the Holy Spirit was multiplied' (Acts 9:31)."[2] Paul and Peter both use the fear of the Lord as a motive to holy and righteous living.[3] The example of the Lord Jesus himself, of whom Isaiah said, "and he will delight in the fear of the Lord" (11:3), should put the question beyond all doubt. If Jesus in his humanity delighted in the fear of God, surely we need to give serious thought to cultivating this attitude in our lives.

Some of the aversion to the phrase "fear of God" may be due to a misunderstanding of its meaning. The Bible uses the term "fear of God" in two distinct ways: that of anxious dread, and that of veneration, reverence, and awe. Fear as anxious dread is produced by the realization of God's impending judgment upon sin. When Adam sinned he hid from God because he was afraid. Although this aspect of the fear of God should characterize every unsaved person who lives each day as an object of God's wrath, it seldom does. Paul's concluding indictment of ungodly mankind was, "There is no fear of God before their eyes" (Romans 3:18).

The Christian has been delivered from fear of the wrath of God (see 1 John 4:18). But the Christian has not been delivered from the *discipline* of God against his sinful conduct, and in this sense he still fears God. He works out his salvation with fear and trembling (Philippians 2:12); he lives his life as a stranger here in reverent fear (1 Peter 1:17).

For the child of God, however, the primary meaning of the fear of God is veneration and honor, reverence and awe. Murray says this fear is the soul of godliness. It is the attitude that elicits from our hearts adoration and love, reverence and honor. It focuses not upon the wrath of God but upon the majesty, holiness, and transcendent glory of God. It may be likened to the awe an ordinary but loyal citizen would feel in the close presence of his earthly king, though such awe for an earthly potentate can only distantly approximate the awe we should feel toward God, the blessed and only Ruler, the King of kings and Lord of lords.

The angelic beings of Isaiah's vision in chapter 6 demonstrated this awe when, with two of their wings, they covered their faces in the presence of the exalted Lord. We see this same awe in Isaiah himself and in Peter when they each realized they were in the presence of a holy God. We see it most vividly in the reaction of the beloved disciple John in Revelation 1:17, when he saw his Master in all of his heavenly glory and majesty, and fell at his feet as though dead.

It is impossible to be devoted to God if one's heart is not filled with the fear of God. It is this profound sense of veneration and honor, reverence and awe that draws forth from our hearts the worship and adoration that characterizes true devotion to God. The reverent, godly Christian sees God first in his transcendent glory, majesty, and holiness before he sees him in his love, mercy, and grace.

There is a healthy tension that exists in the godly person's heart between the reverential awe of God in his glory and the childlike confidence in God as heavenly Father. Without this tension, a Christian's filial confidence can easily degenerate into presumption.

One of the more serious sins of Christians today may well be the almost flippant familiarity with which we often address God in prayer. None of the godly men of the Bible ever adopted the casual manner we often do. They always addressed God with reverence. The same writer who tells us that we have confidence to enter the Most Holy Place, the throne room of God, also tells us that we should worship God acceptably with reverence and awe, "for our God is a consuming fire" (Hebrews 10:19 and 12:28-29). The same Paul who tells us that the Holy Spirit dwelling within us causes us to cry, "*Abba*, Father," also tells us that this same God lives in "unapproachable light" (Romans 8:15 and 1 Timothy 6:16).

In our day we must begin to recover a sense of awe and profound reverence for God. We must begin to view him once again in the infinite majesty that alone belongs to him who is the Creator and Supreme Ruler of the entire universe. There is an infinite gap in worth and dignity between God the Creator and man the creature, even though man has been created in the image of God. The fear of God is a heartfelt recognition of this gap—not a put-down of man, but an exaltation of God.

Even the redeemed in heaven fear the Lord. In Revelation 15:3-4, they sing triumphantly the song of Moses the servant of God and the song of the Lamb:

> Great and marvelous are your deeds,
>   Lord God Almighty.
> Just and true are your ways,
>   King of the ages.
> Who will not fear you, O Lord,
>   and bring glory to your name?
> For you alone are holy.
> All nations will come
>   and worship before you,
> for your righteous acts have been revealed.

Note the focus of their veneration upon God's attributes of power, justice, and holiness. It is these attributes, which particularly set forth the majesty of God, that should elicit from our hearts a reverence for him. This same reverence was drawn forth from the children of Israel when they saw the great power the Lord displayed against the Egyptians. Exodus 14:31 says, "the people feared the Lord and put their trust in him and in Moses his servant." Along with Moses they sang a song of worship and gratitude. The heart of that song is found in 15:11: "Who among the gods is like you, O Lord? Who is like you—majestic in holiness, awesome in glory, working wonders?" To fear God is to confess his absolute uniqueness—to acknowledge his majesty, holiness, awesomeness, glory, and power.

Words fail us to describe the infinite glory of God portrayed in the Bible. And even that portrayal is dim and vague, for now we see but a poor reflection of him. But one day we will see him face to face, and then we will fear him in the fullest sense of that word. No wonder, then, that with that day in view, Peter tells us to live holy and godly lives now. God is in the process of preparing us for heaven, to dwell with him for eternity. So he desires that we grow in both holiness and godliness. He wants us to be like him and to reverence and adore him for all eternity. We must be learning to do this now.

In our day we seem to have magnified the love of God almost to the exclusion of the fear of God. Because of this preoccupation we are not honoring God and reverencing him as we should. We should magnify the love of God; but although we revel in his love and mercy, we must never lose sight of his majesty and his holiness.

Not only will a right concept of the fear of God cause us to worship God aright, it will also regulate our conduct. As John Murray says, "What or whom we worship determines our behavior."[4] The Reverend Albert N. Martin has said that the essential ingredients of the fear of God are (1) correct concepts of the character of God, (2) a pervasive sense of the presence of God, and (3) a constant awareness of our obligation to God.[5] If we have some comprehension of God's infinite holiness and his hatred of sin, coupled with this pervasive sense of God's presence in all of our actions, yes, even our thoughts, then such a fear of God must influence and regulate our conduct. Just as obedience to the Lord is an indication of our love for him, so is it also a proof of our fear of God. "[You shall] fear the Lord your God as long as you live by keeping all his decrees and commands . . .'' (Deuteronomy 6:2).

Leviticus 19 contains a series of laws and regulations for the nation of Israel to observe in the promised land. This is the chapter from which Jesus quoted the well-known second commandment of love, ''Love your neighbor as yourself'' (verse 18; see also Matthew 22:39). The expression ''I am the Lord'' or ''I am the Lord your God'' appears sixteen times in Leviticus 19. Through this frequent repetition of his sacred name, God reminds the people of Israel that their obedience to his laws and regulations is to flow out of a reverence and fear of him.

The fear of God should provide a primary motivation for, as well as result in, obedience to him. If we truly reverence God we will obey him, since every act of disobedience is an affront to his dignity and majesty.

Gripped by God's love

Only the God-fearing Christian can truly appreciate the love of God. He sees the infinite gulf between a holy God and a sinful creature, and the love that bridged that gulf through the death of the Lord Jesus Christ. God's love for us is many-faceted, but he supremely demonstrated it by sending his Son to die for our sins. All other aspects of his love are secondary, and in fact are made possible for us through the death of Christ.

The apostle John says, ''God is love'' (1 John 4:8). He explains this statement by saying, ''This is how God showed his love among us: He sent his one and only Son into the world that we might live through him. This is love: not that we loved God, but that he loved us and sent his Son as an atoning sacrifice for our sins" (1 John 4:9-10). The *New International Version* of the Bible gives as a marginal rendering for "atoning sacrifice" the phrase, "as the one who would turn aside his wrath, taking away" our sins.

The truly godly person never forgets that he was at one time an object of God's holy and just wrath. He never forgets that Christ Jesus came into the world to save sinners—and he feels along with Paul that he is himself the worst of sinners. But then as he looks to the cross he sees that Jesus was his atoning sacrifice. He sees that Jesus bore his sins in his own body, and that the wrath of God—the wrath which he, a sinner, should have borne—was expended completely and totally upon the holy Son of God. And in this view of Calvary, he sees the love of God.

The love of God has no meaning apart from Calvary. And Calvary has no meaning apart from the holy and just wrath of God. Jesus did not die just to give us peace and a purpose in life; he died to save us from the wrath of God. He died to reconcile us to a holy God who was alienated from us because of our sin. He died to ransom us from the penalty of sin—the punishment of everlasting destruction, shut out from the presence of the Lord. He died that we, the just objects of God's wrath, should become, by his grace, heirs of God and co-heirs with him.

How much we appreciate God's love is conditioned by how deeply we fear him. The more we see God in his infinite majesty, holiness, and transcendent glory, the more we will gaze with wonder and amazement upon his love poured out at Calvary. But it is also true that the deeper our perception of God's love to us in Christ, the more profound our reverence and awe of him. We must see God in the glory of all his attributes—his goodness as well as his holiness—if we are to ascribe to him the glory and honor and reverence that is due him. The psalmist caught this truth when he said to God, "If you, O Lord, kept a record of sins, O Lord, who could stand? But with you there is forgiveness; therefore you are feared" (Psalm 130:3-4). He worshiped God with reverence and awe because of his forgiveness. In our practice of godliness, then, we must seek to grow both in the fear of God and in an ever-increasing comprehension of the love of God. These two elements together form the foundation of our devotion to God.

This awareness of God's love for us in Christ must be *personalized* in order for it to become one of the solid foundational corners of our "triangle of devotion" to God. It is not enough to believe that God loved the world. I must be gripped by the realization that God loves *me*, a specific person. It is this awareness of his individual love that draws out our hearts in devotion to him.

There was a period in my early Christian life when my concept of God's love was little more than a logical deduction: God loves the world; I am a part of the world; therefore, God loves me. It was as if God's love were a big umbrella to protect us all from his judgment against sin, and I was under the umbrella along with thousands of other people. There was nothing particularly personal about it. Then one day I realized, "God loves *me*! Christ died for *me*."

Our awareness of God's love for us must also be constantly growing. As we mature in our Christian lives we are increasingly aware of God's holiness and our own sinfulness. In Paul's first letter to Timothy he reflects upon God's mercy in appointing him to the gospel ministry. He recalls that he once was a blasphemer and a persecutor and a violent man. This description no longer applies to Paul; it is all past tense. But as he continues to reflect upon the grace of God, he slips, almost unconsciously it seems, into the present tense of his experience. "Christ Jesus came into the world to save sinners—of whom I am the worst" (1:15). He is no longer thinking about his past as a persecutor of Christ. Now he is thinking about his present daily experience as a believer who falls short of the will of God for him. He doesn't think about other Christians, whom we know were way behind Paul in their devotion to God and their attainment of godly character. Paul never wastes time trying to feel good about himself by comparing himself favorably with less mature Christians. He compares himself with God's standard, and he consequently sees himself as the worst of sinners.

Through this present sense of his sinfulness Paul sees God's love for him. The more he grows in his knowledge of God's perfect will, the more he sees his own sinfulness, and the more he comprehends God's love in sending Christ to die for him. And the more he sees God's love, the more his heart reaches out in adoring devotion to the One who loved him so.

If God's love for us is to be a solid foundation stone of devotion, we must realize that his love is *entirely of grace*, that it rests completely upon the work of Jesus Christ and flows to us through our union with him. Because of this basis his love can never change, regardless of what we do. In our daily experience, we have all sorts of spiritual ups and downs—sin, failure, discouragement, all of which tend to make us question God's love. That is because we keep thinking that God's love is somehow conditional. We are afraid to believe his love is based entirely upon the finished work of Christ for us.

Deep down in our souls we must get hold of the wonderful truth that our spiritual failures do not affect God's love for us one iota—that his love for us does not fluctuate according to our experience. We must be gripped by the truth that we are accepted by God and loved by God for the sole reason that we are united to his beloved Son. As the *King James Version* translates Ephesians 1:6, ''he hath made us accepted in the beloved.''

This is why Paul could rejoice so greatly in the love of God. Listen to the triumphant ring of his voice in Romans 8 as he asks these questions:

''If God is for us, who can be against us?''

''Who will bring any charge against those whom God has chosen?''

''Who is he that condemns?''

''Who shall separate us from the love of Christ?''

Then hear his exultant conclusion as he says, ''For I am convinced that . . . [nothing] . . . will be able to separate us from the love of God that is in Christ Jesus our Lord.''

Does this apprehension of God's personal, unconditional love for us in Christ lead to careless living? Not at all. Rather, such an awareness of his love stimulates in us an increased devotion to him. And this devotion is active; it is not just a warm, affectionate feeling toward God.

Paul testified that Christ's love for us compelled him to live not for himself, but for him who died for us and rose again (2 Corinthians 5:14-15). The word for "compel" which Paul used is a very strong verb. It means to press in on all sides and to impel or force one to a certain course of action. Probably not many Christians can identify with Paul in this depth of his motivation, but this surely should be our goal. This is the constraining force God's love is intended to have upon us.

John speaks similarly of the constraining force of God's love when he says, "We love because he first loved us" (1 John 4:19). Whether it is love for God or love for other people that John had in mind, both are prompted by the realization of God's love for us.

So we see that devotion to God begins with the fear of God—with a biblical view of his majesty and holiness that elicits a reverence and awe of him. And then we see that the fear of God leads naturally to an apprehension of the love of God for us as shown in the atoning death of Jesus Christ. As we contemplate God more and more in his majesty, holiness, and love, we will be progressively led to the apex of the triangle of devotion—the desire for God himself.

A thirst for God

True godliness engages our affections and awakens within us a desire to enjoy God's presence and fellowship. It produces a longing for God himself. The writer of Psalm 42 vividly expressed this longing when he exclaimed, "As the deer pants for streams of water, so my soul pants for you, O God. My soul thirsts for God, for the living God. When can I go and meet with God?'' What could be more intense than a hunted deer's thirst for water? The psalmist does not hesitate to use this picture to illustrate the intensity of his own desire for God's presence and fellowship.

David also expresses this intense desire for God: ''One thing I ask of the Lord, this is what I seek: that I may dwell in the house of the Lord all the days of my life, to gaze upon the beauty of the Lord and to seek him in his temple'' (Psalm 27:4). David yearned intensely for God himself that he might enjoy his presence and his beauty. Since God is a spirit, his beauty obviously refers not to a physical appearance but to his attributes. David enjoyed dwelling upon the majesty and greatness, the holiness and goodness of God. But David did more than contemplate the beauty of God's attributes. He sought God himself, for elsewhere he says, ''earnestly I seek you; my soul thirsts for you, my body longs for you . . .'' (Psalm 63:1).

The apostle Paul also experienced this longing for God: ''I want to know Christ . . .'' (Philippians 3:10). The *Amplified Bible* forcefully catches the intensity of Paul's desire in this passage: ''[For my determined purpose is] that I may know Him—that I may progressively become more deeply and intimately acquainted with Him, perceiving and recognizing and understanding [the wonders of His person] more strongly and more clearly.'' This is the heartbeat of the godly person. As he contemplates God in the awesomeness of his infinite majesty, power, and holiness, and then as he dwells upon the riches of his mercy and grace poured out at Calvary, his heart is captivated by this One who could love him so. He is satisfied with God alone, but he is never satisfied with his present experience of God. He always yearns for more.

Perhaps this idea of a desire for God sounds strange to many Christians today. We understand the thought of serving God, of being busy in his work. We may even have a "quiet time" when we read the Bible and pray. But the idea of longing for God himself, of wanting to deeply enjoy his fellowship and his presence, may seem a bit too mystical, almost bordering on fanaticism. We prefer our Christianity to be more practical.

Yet who could be more practical than Paul? Who was more involved in the struggles of daily living than David? Still, with all their responsibilities, both Paul and David yearned to experience more fellowship with the living God. The Bible indicates that this is God's plan for us, from its earliest pages right through to the end. In the third chapter of Genesis God walks in the garden, calling out for Adam that he might have fellowship with him. In Revelation 21, when John sees the vision of the new Jerusalem coming down from heaven, he hears the voice of God say, "Now the dwelling of God is with men, and he will live with them" (verse 3). For all of eternity God plans to have fellowship with his people.

And during our present day, Jesus still says to us as he did to the church at Laodicea, "Here I am! I stand at the door and knock. If anyone hears my voice and opens the door, I will come in and eat with him, and he with me" (Revelation 3:20). In the culture of

John's day, to share a meal meant to have fellowship, so Jesus is inviting us to open our hearts to him that we may fellowship with him. He desires that we come to know him better; therefore, the desire and yearning for God is something that he plants within our hearts.

In the life of the godly person, this desire for God produces an aura of warmth. Godliness is never austere and cold. Such an idea comes from a false sense of legalistic morality that is erroneously called godliness. The person who spends time with God radiates his glory in a manner that is always warm and inviting, never cold and forbidding.

This longing for God also produces a desire to glorify God and to please him. In the same breath, Paul expresses the desire to know Christ as well as to be like him. This is God's ultimate objective for us and is the object of the Spirit's work in us. In Isaiah 26:9, the prophet proclaims his desire for the Lord in words very similar to the psalmist's: "My soul yearns for you in the night; in the morning my spirit longs for you." Note that immediately before this expression of desire for the Lord, he expresses a desire for his glory: "Your name and renown are the desire of our hearts" (verse 8). Renown has to do with one's reputation, fame and eminence—or in God's case, with his glory. The prophet could not separate in his heart his desire for God's glory and his desire for God himself. These two yearnings go hand in hand.

This is devotion to God—the fear of God, which is an attitude of reverence and awe, veneration and honor toward him, coupled with an apprehension deep within our souls of the love of God for us, demonstrated preeminently in the atoning death of

Christ. These two attitudes complement and reinforce each other, producing within our souls an intense desire for this One who is so awesome in his glory and majesty and yet so condescending in his love and mercy.

Notes

1. John Murray, *Principles of Conduct* (Grand Rapids, Mich.: Eerdmans, 1978), page 229.
2. Murray, page 230.
3. See, for example, 2 Corinthians 7:1, Ephesians 5:21, Colossians 3:22, and 1 Peter 1:17. The *New International Version* of the Bible uses the word *reverence* for "fear" in some of these passages. It is, however, the same Greek word translated as "fear" in other places.
4. Murray, page 231.
5. Albert N. Martin, cassette tape series, "The Fear of God" (Essex Fells, N.J.: The Trinity Pulpit). This series consists of nine messages on the fear of God. I highly recommend it to those who wish to pursue this subject in greater detail. I am indebted to the Reverend Martin for the definition of the fear of God used in this chapter.

3
Train Yourself to Be Godly

HAVE NOTHING TO DO WITH
GODLESS MYTHS AND OLD WIVES'
TALES; RATHER, TRAIN YOURSELF
TO BE GODLY.

1 Timothy 4:7

The apostle Paul did not take for granted the godliness of his spiritual son Timothy. Though Timothy had been his companion and co-laborer for a number of years, Paul still felt it necessary to write to him, "train yourself to be godly." And if Timothy needed this encouragement, then surely we also need it today.

In urging Timothy to train himself in godliness, Paul borrowed a term from the realm of athletics. The verb which is variously translated in different versions of the Bible as "exercise," "discipline," or "train" originally referred to the training of young athletes for participation in the competitive games of the day. Then it took on a more general meaning of training or discipline of either the body or the mind in a particular skill.

41

Principles for training

There are several principles in Paul's exhortation to Timothy to train himself to be godly that are applicable to us today. The first is *personal responsibility*. Paul said, "Train yourself." Timothy was personally responsible for his progress in godliness. He was not to trust the Lord for that progress and then relax, though he certainly understood that any progress he made was only through divine enablement. He would have understood that he was to work out this particular aspect of his salvation in confidence that God was at work in him. But he would get Paul's message that he must work at this matter of godliness; he must *pursue* it.

We Christians may be very disciplined and industrious in our business, our studies, our home, or even our ministry, but we tend to be lazy when it comes to exercise in our own spiritual lives. We would much rather pray, "Lord, make me godly," and expect him to "pour" some godliness into our souls in some mysterious way. God does in fact work in a mysterious way to make us godly, but he does not do this apart from the fulfillment of our own personal responsibility. We are to train ourselves to be godly.

The second principle in Paul's exhortation is that *the object of this training was growth* in Timothy's personal spiritual life. Elsewhere Paul encourages Timothy to progress in his ministry, but the objective here is Timothy's own devotion to God and the conduct arising from that devotion. Even though he was an experienced, well-qualified Christian minister, Timothy still needed to grow in the essential areas of godliness—the fear of God, the comprehension of the love of God, and the desire for the presence and fellowship of God.

I have been in a full-time Christian ministry for well over twenty-five years and have served both overseas and in the United States. During this time I have met many talented and capable Christians, but I think I have met fewer godly Christians. The emphasis of our age is on serving God, accomplishing things for God. Enoch was a preacher of righteousness in a day of gross ungodliness, but God saw fit that the brief account of his life emphasized that he walked with God. What are we training ourselves for? Are we training ourselves only in Christian activity, as good as that may be, or are we training ourselves first of all in godliness?

The third principle in Paul's words of exhortation to Timothy is the importance of *minimum characteristics necessary for training*. Many of us have watched various Olympic competitions on television, and as the commentators have given us the backgrounds of the various athletes, we become aware of certain irreducible minimums in the training of all Olympic competitors. It is very likely that Paul had these minimum characteristics in mind as he compared physical training with training in godliness

The cost of commitment

The first of these irreducible minimums is *commitment*. No one makes it to the level of Olympic, or even national, competition without a commitment to pay the price of rigorous, daily training. And similarly, no one ever becomes godly without a commitment to pay the price of the daily spiritual training which

God has designed for our growth in godliness.

The concept of commitment occurs repeatedly throughout the Bible. It is found in David's cry to God, "earnestly I seek you" (Psalm 63:1). It is found in God's promise to the captives in Babylon, "You will seek me and find me when you seek me with all your heart" (Jeremiah 29:13). It occurs in Paul's pressing on to take hold of that for which Christ Jesus took hold of him (Philippians 3:12). It lies behind such exhortations as "Make every effort . . . to be holy" (Hebrews 12:14), and "make every effort to add to your faith . . . godliness" (2 Peter 1:5-7). None of this seeking, pressing on, or making every effort will occur without commitment on our part.

There is a price to godliness, and godliness is never on sale. It never comes cheaply or easily. The verb *train*, which Paul deliberately chose, implies persevering, painstaking, diligent effort. He was well aware of the total commitment those young athletes made to win a crown that would not last. And as he thought of the crown that would last—the godliness that has value for all things, both in the present life and the life to come—he urged Timothy, and he urges us today, to make the kind of commitment necessary to train ourselves to be godly.

Learning from a skilled teacher

The second irreducible minimum in training is *a competent teacher or coach*. No athlete, regardless of how much natural ability he has, can make it to the Olympics without a skillful coach who holds him to the highest standard of excellence and sees and corrects every minor fault. In the same way we cannot train ourselves to be godly without the teaching and training ministry of the Holy Spirit. He holds us to the highest standard of spiritual excellence as he teaches, rebukes, corrects, and trains us. But he teaches and trains us through his word. Therefore we must consistently expose ourselves to the teaching of the word of God if we are to grow in godliness.

In Titus 1:1 Paul refers to "the knowledge of the truth that leads to godliness." We cannot grow in godliness without the knowledge of this truth. This truth is to be found only in the Bible, but it is not just academic knowledge of Bible facts. It is spiritual knowledge taught by the Holy Spirit as he applies the truth of God to our hearts.

There is a type of religious knowledge that is actually detrimental to training in godliness. It is the knowledge that puffs up with spiritual pride. The Corinthian Christians had this kind of knowledge. They knew that an idol was nothing and that eating food sacrificed to an idol was a matter of spiritual indifference. But they did not know about their responsibility to love their weaker brother. Only the Holy Spirit imparts that type of knowledge—the type that leads to godliness.

It is possible to be very orthodox in one's doctrine and very upright in one's behavior and still not be godly. Many people are orthodox and upright, but they are not devoted to God; they are devoted to their orthodoxy and their standards of moral conduct.

Only the Holy Spirit can pry us loose from such positions of false confidence, so we must sincerely look to him for his training ministry as we seek to grow in godliness. We must spend much time in exposure to his word, since it is his means of teaching us. But this exposure must be accompanied by a sense of deep humility regarding our ability to learn spiritual truth and a sense of utter dependence upon his ministry in our hearts.

Practice, and more practice

The third irreducible minimum in the training process is *practice*. It is practice that puts feet to the commitment and applies the teaching of the coach. It is practice, where the skill is developed, that makes the athlete competitive in his sport. And it is the practice of godliness that enables us to become godly Christians. There is no shortcut to Olympic-level skill, there is no shortcut to godliness. It is the day in and day out faithfulness to the means which God has appointed and which the Holy Spirit uses that will enable us to grow in godliness. We must *practice* godliness, just as the athlete practices his particular sport.

We must practice the fear of God, for example, if we are to grow in that aspect of godly devotion. If we agree with the Reverend Martin that the essential elements of the fear of God are correct concepts of his character, a pervasive sense of his presence, and a constant awareness of our responsibility to him, then we must work at filling our minds with the biblical expressions of these truths and applying them in our lives until we are transformed into God-fearing people.

If we become convinced that humility is a trait of godly character, then we will frequently meditate upon such Scripture passages as Isaiah 57:15 and 66:1-2, where God himself extols humility. We will pray over them, asking the Holy Spirit to apply them in our lives to make us truly humble. This is the practice of godliness. It is not some ethereal exercise. It is practical, down-to-earth, and even a bit grubby at times as the Holy Spirit works on us. But it is always rewarding as we see the Spirit transforming us more and more into godly people.

Using the word of God

It is evident that the word of God plays a crucial role in our growth in godliness. A prominent part of our practice of godliness, therefore, will be our time in the word of God. How we spend that time varies according to the method of intake. The Navigators use the five fingers of the hand as mental pegs on which to hang the five methods of intake of the word of God—hearing, reading, studying, memorizing, and meditating. These methods are important for godliness and need to be considered one by one.

The most common method of scriptural intake is *hearing* the word of God taught to us by our pastors and teachers. We are living in a day when this method tends to be lightly regarded by many people as being a somewhat ineffective means of learning spiritual truth. This is a serious error. The Lord Jesus Christ himself has given to his church people who are gifted to teach us the truths of his word, to remind us of the lessons we are prone to forget, and to exhort us to constancy in application. We need to heed those whom he has given to us for this purpose.

None of us ever becomes so spiritually self-sufficient that he does not need to hear the word taught by others. And most of us do not have the

ability or the time to search out on our own the
"whole will of God" (Acts 20:27). We need to sit
under the regular teaching of a man gifted by God
and trained to expound the word of God to us.

One reason the hearing of the word of God has
fallen into such low esteem is that we do not obey
God's teaching in Revelation 1:3—"blessed are
those who hear it and take to heart what is written in
it." Too often today we listen to be entertained instead of instructed, to be moved emotionally rather
than moved to obedience. We do not take to heart
what we hear and apply it in our daily lives.

We present-day Christians are hardly different
from the Jews of Ezekiel's time, of whom God said,
"My people come to you, as they usually do, and sit
before you to listen to your words, but they do not put
them into practice" (Ezekiel 33:31). God goes on to
tell Ezekiel that to his audience, Ezekiel is nothing
more than a singer with a beautiful voice who plays an
instrument well. To the Jews he was just an enter-
tainer, because they had no intention of putting into
practice what they heard.

The type of hearing of the word that God commends is illustrated by the Berean Christians, who
"received the message with great eagerness and examined the Scriptures every day to see if what Paul
said was true" (Acts 17:11). They did not hear and
forget; they did not listen just to be entertained. They
realized eternal issues were at stake, so they listened,
studied, and applied. Considering that they probably did not have their own personal copies of the
Scriptures, their studying of Paul's teaching is
remarkable. It is a rebuke to us today, who scarcely

remember beyond the church door what we heard in the sermon on Sunday morning.

We have already considered briefly the thought expressed in Titus 1:1—it is the knowledge of the truth that leads to godliness. But that is not all the verse says. In the same passage, Paul says he is an apostle of Jesus Christ for the purpose of furthering the faith of God's elect and their knowledge of the truth that leads to godliness. Paul was called to be a teacher for the express purpose of promoting faith and godliness among God's elect. God called Paul to that task, and he calls pastors and teachers today for the same purpose. But if we are to profit from their ministry so that we grow in the knowledge of the truth that leads to godliness, we must hear their word as the Berean Christians heard Paul—with great eagerness and an intent to obey.

The second method of scriptural intake is *reading* the Bible ourselves. Through Bible reading we have the opportunity to learn directly from the Master Teacher, the Holy Spirit. As helpful and profitable as it is to learn from the teaching of others, there is an unmatched joy in having the Holy Spirit speak to us directly from the pages of his word.

We have already seen that Enoch walked with God, which implies that he enjoyed personal communion with God. Bible reading enables us, too, to enjoy communion with God as he speaks to us from his word, encouraging us, instructing us, and revealing himself to us. It was said of Moses that "the Lord would speak to [him] face to face, as a man speaks with his friend" (Exodus 33:11). Today we do not have that particular privilege, but we can enjoy the same effect as God speaks to us during our times of personal Bible reading. Our practice of godliness would be very incomplete without a regular Bible reading program of some type.

A second value of Bible reading is the opportunity to gain an overall perspective of the entire Bible. No pastor could—or should—preach through the Bible in the short space of a year or two. But all of us can *read* through the entire Bible in a year. Many Bible reading plans are available to help us do so. As we read through the Bible, the various pieces of spiritual truth begin to fit together. The book of Hebrews doesn't make sense unless one is at least knowledgeable of the Old Testament priesthood and sacrificial system. The New Testament writers' many allusions to the Old Testament would remain a mystery unless we had read the passages in their original setting. The doctrine of original sin through Adam, as taught by Paul in Romans 5, cannot be understood apart from a knowledge of the events recorded in Genesis 3.

Without a reading program of the entire Bible, we would be not only spiritually ignorant, but spiritually impoverished. Who can fail to learn from Abraham's faith, David's love for God, Daniel's righteousness, and Job's trial? How can we become godly without the heartbeat of the Psalms and the practical wisdom of Proverbs? Where better can we learn of both the majesty and the faithfulness of God than from the prophet Isaiah? If we are not periodically reading through the Bible, we will miss these outstanding passages in the Old Testament as well as others in the New Testament.

All Scripture is profitable for us, even passages that seem so difficult to understand. We can choose from among various Bible reading programs to help us maintain consistency in our reading and understand the more difficult passages.[1]

The third method of Bible intake is *studying* the Scriptures. Reading gives us breadth, but study gives us depth. The value of Bible study lies in the opportunity to dig more deeply into a passage or topic than we can do in Bible reading. Greater diligence and mental intensity are required for study, in which we analyze a passage, compare Scripture with Scripture, ask questions, make observations, and finally organize the fruit of our study into some kind of logical presentation. The discipline of writing down our study material helps to clarify our thoughts. All of this strengthens our knowledge of the truth and helps us to grow in godliness.

Every Christian should be a student of the Bible. The Hebrew Christians were rebuked, because although they should have been able to teach others they still needed to be taught the elementary truths of God's word. They needed milk, not solid food! Unfortunately, many of us are like those Christians.

There are numerous methods of Bible study available for every level of student. There are certain principles that should be applied, however, whatever method is used. These principles are set forth in Proverbs 2:1-5. Note the verbs that have been italicized for emphasis:

My son, if you *accept* my words and *store up* my commands within you, *turning* your ear to

wisdom and *applying* your heart to understanding,
and if you *call out* for insight and *cry aloud* for
understanding, and if you *look* for it as for silver
and *search* for it as for hidden treasure, then you
will understand the fear of the Lord and find the
knowledge of God.

The verbs that are italicized give us an idea of the
principles involved in Bible study, such as,

- teachability—accept my words
- intent to obey—store up my commands
- mental discipline—apply your heart
- prayerful dependence—call out, cry aloud
- diligent perseverance—search as for hidden
treasure.

The results of applying these principles in Bible
study are located in verse 5: "Then you will understand the fear of the Lord and find the knowledge of
God"—two of the concepts essential in our devotion
to God. If we are to train ourselves to be godly we
must give Bible study priority in our lives.

Where can we find the time for quality Bible
study? I once heard that question asked of a chief of
surgery in a large hospital. Twenty-five years later, his
answer continues to challenge me. He looked his
questioner squarely in the eye and said, "You always
find time for what is important to you." How important is the practice of godliness to you? Is it important
enough to take priority over television, books, magazines, recreation, and a score of activities that we all
somehow find time to engage in? Once again we are
brought face to face with that key element of training
we discussed earlier—commitment.

Memorization of key passages is a fourth method of scriptural intake. Without doubt the classic verse for Scripture memorization is Psalm 119:11: "I have hidden your word in my heart that I might not sin against you." The word that is translated in verse 11 as "hidden" is elsewhere translated as "stored up," a phrase which is more descriptive of the actual meaning. In Proverbs 7:1, for example, Solomon says, "My son . . . *store up* my commands within you," and in Proverbs 10:14 he says, "Wise men *store up* knowledge." In Psalm 31:19 David speaks of the goodness which God has *stored up* for those who fear him. From these passages it is clear that the central idea of the psalmist in Psalm 119:11 was that of storing up God's word in his heart against a time of future need—a time when he would encounter temptation and would be kept from that temptation by the word of God.

But the word of God stored in the heart does more than keep us from sin. It enables us to grow in every area of the Christian life. Specifically for our practice of godliness it enables us to grow in our devotion to God and in the Godlike character that makes our lives pleasing to him.[2]

The fifth method for taking in God's word is *meditation*. The word *meditate* as used in the Old Testament literally means to murmur or to mutter and, by implication, to talk to oneself.[3] When we meditate on the Scriptures we talk to ourselves about them, turning over in our minds the meanings, the implications, and the applications to our own lives.

Though we use Psalm 119:11 in connection with Scripture memorization, it may be more supportive of the practice of meditation. The psalmist says God's word was stored up in his *heart*—his inmost being. Bare memorization only gets the Scriptures into our minds. Meditation on those same Scriptures opens our understanding, engages our affections, and addresses our wills. This is the process of storing up the word in our hearts. But if the process of storing up Scripture applies primarily to meditation, it is also true that memorization is the first step to meditation. Meditation on the word of God is commanded in Joshua 1:8 and commended in Psalm 1:2. Both verses speak of meditation *day and night*, not just when we are having our quiet time. It is impossible to meditate on Scripture day and night without some form of Scripture memorization.

In chapter one we defined godliness as devotion to God which results in a life that is pleasing to God. If we had to select one chapter of the Bible that portrays the heartbeat of the godly person, it would probably be Psalm 119. In all but two of its 176 verses, the writer relates his life to the word of God and to the God behind that word. It is always *your* law, *your* statutes, *your* desires, *your* precepts, etc. To the psalmist, the law of God was not the cold commands of some far-off deity, but the living word of the God whom he loved, sought, and yearned to please.

Walking with God involves communion with God. His word is absolutely necessary and central to our communion with him. Pleasing God requires knowing his will—how he wants us to live, what he wants us to do. His word is the only means by which he communicates that will to us. It is impossible to practice godliness without a constant, consistent, and balanced intake of the word of God in our lives.

The intake of the word is our foundational means of practicing godliness, but it is not our only means. In the next chapter we will consider how to develop a devotion to God. In subsequent chapters we will consider how to grow in some individual traits of godly character, including a look at some practical steps we can take in the practice of godliness.

The nature of training

Paul said, "Train yourself to be godly." You and I are responsible to train ourselves. We are dependent upon God for his divine enablement, but we are responsible; we are not passive in this process. Our objective in this process is godliness—not proficiency in ministry, but God-centered devotion and Godlike character. We do want to develop proficiency in ministry, but for training in godliness we want to focus on our relationship with God.

Training in godliness requires commitment, the teaching ministry of the Holy Spirit through his word, and practice on our part. Are we prepared to accept our responsibility and make that commitment? As we ponder that question let us remember, "godliness has value for all things, holding promise for both the present life and the life to come," and "godliness with contentment is great gain" (1 Timothy 4:8 and 6:6).

Notes
1. One of the best aids to daily Bible reading is *The Daily Walk*, available free upon request from The Navigators Daily Walk, P.O. Box 6000, Colorado Springs, Colorado 80934. This publication provides

both a program for reading through the Bible as well as short explanatory notes on each day's reading portion.

2. Information on materials for Bible study and Scripture memorization may be obtained from NavPress, P.O. Box 6000, Colorado Springs, Colorado 80934.

3. William Wilson, *Wilson's Old Testament Word Studies* (MacLean, Va.: MacDonald Publ. Co., n.d.), page 271.

4
Seeking a Deeper Devotion

I SEEK YOU WITH ALL MY HEART;
DO NOT LET ME STRAY FROM
YOUR COMMANDS.

Psalm 119:10

Scripture defines unbelievers as totally godless. Paul tells the Romans that they have no fear of God, are hostile to him, are unwilling to submit to his law, and are unable to please him. This is just as true of the morally upright unbeliever as it is of the most corrupt profligate. The former worships a god of his own mind, not the God of the Bible. When confronted with the claims of the Sovereign God of the Universe, he often reacts with greater hostility than an unbeliever living in open sin.

At the time of our salvation, God through his Holy Spirit deals with this godless spirit within us. He gives us a new heart and moves us to obey him, he gives us a singleness of heart and inspires us to fear him, and he pours out his love into our hearts so that

57

we begin to comprehend his love for us. All of this is bound up in the blessings of the new birth, so we may safely say that all Christians possess, at least in embryonic form, a basic devotion to God. It is impossible to be a Christian and not have it. The work of the Holy Spirit at regeneration assures this. God has given us everything we need for life and godliness.

But though all of us as Christians possess a basic God-centeredness as an integral part of our spiritual lives, we must grow in this devotion to God. We are to train ourselves to be godly; we are to make every effort to add godliness to our faith. To grow in godliness is to grow both in our devotion to God and in our likeness to his character.

In chapter two we illustrated devotion to God by a triangle whose three points represent the fear of God, the love of God, and the desire for God. To grow in our devotion to God is to grow in each of these three areas. And as the triangle is equal on all three sides, so we should seek to grow equally in all of these areas; otherwise our devotion becomes unbalanced.

To seek to grow in the fear of God, for example, without also growing in our comprehension of his love can cause us to begin to view God as far-off and austere. Or to seek to grow in our awareness of the love of God without also growing in our reverence and awe of him can cause us to view God as a permissive and indulgent heavenly Father who does not deal with our sin. This latter unbalanced view is prevalent in our society today. That is why many Christians are calling for a renewed emphasis on the biblical teaching of the fear of God.

A crucial characteristic of our growth in godly

devotion, then, must be a balanced approach to all three of the essential elements of devotion: fear, love, and desire. Another crucial characteristic must be a *vital dependence upon the Holy Spirit* to bring about this growth. The principle of Christian ministry that Paul states in 1 Corinthians 3:7, "neither he who plants nor he who waters is anything, but only God, who makes things grow," is just as true as a principle of growth in godliness. We must plant and water through whatever means of grace God has given us, but only God can make godly devotion increase within our hearts.

Praying for growth

We express this vital dependence on God by praying that he will cause us to grow in our devotion to him. David prayed, "give me an undivided heart, that I may fear your name" (Psalm 86:11). Paul prayed that the Ephesian Christians might be able to grasp how wide and long and high and deep is the love of Christ (Ephesians 3:16-19). And David prayed that he might dwell in the house of the Lord to behold his beauty and to seek him in his temple (Psalm 27:4). Each of these prayers is a recognition that growth in devotion to God is of him.

If we are committed to the practice of godliness, our prayer life will reflect it. We will be regularly asking God to increase our fear of him, to deepen our understanding of his love for us, and to heighten our desire for his fellowship. We would do well, for example, to put the three verses mentioned above, or similar passages, on our list of prayer requests and pray over them regularly.

Meditating on God

We have already discussed the overall importance of the word of God in developing godliness. The word also helps us specifically in the three areas of devotion—the fear of God, the love of God, and the desire for God.

Although all of the Bible should instruct us in the fear of God, I have found there are certain passages that are especially helpful to me in drawing my attention to the majesty and holiness of God—the attributes particularly suited to stimulate our hearts in the fear of God. Here are some passages I refer to frequently:

- Isaiah 6 and Revelation 4—God's holiness
- Isaiah 40—God's greatness
- Psalm 139—God's omniscience and omnipresence
- Revelation 1:10-17 and Revelation 5—the majesty of Christ.

These Scripture selections are intended only as suggestions. You may find others that are more meaningful to you. Use them. The important point is that God uses his word to create in our hearts the sense of reverence and awe of him that causes us to fear him. It is vain to pray for an increase of the fear of God in our hearts without meditating on passages of Scripture that are particularly suited to stimulate that fear.

There are also specific passages that will help us grow in our awareness of God's love for us. Those I find especially helpful are Psalm 103, Isaiah 53, Romans 5:6-11, Ephesians 2:1-10, 2 Corinthians 5:14-21, 1 Timothy 1:15-16, and 1 John 4:9-11.

In commending certain passages of Scripture to

you, I cannot emphasize too strongly, however, that it is not just the bare reading, or even memorizing, of these passages that accomplishes the desired result of growth in godliness. We must meditate on them, but even that is not sufficient. The Holy Spirit must make his word come alive to our hearts to produce the growth, so we must meditate in prayerful dependence upon him to do his work. Neither meditation nor prayer by themselves are sufficient for growth in devotion. We must practice both.

Worshiping God

Still another essential part of our practice of devotion to God is *worship*. By worship I mean the specific act of ascribing to God the glory, majesty, honor, and worthiness which are his. Revelation 4:8-11 and 5:9-14 give us clear illustrations of the worship that goes on in heaven and which should be emulated by us here on earth. I almost always begin my daily quiet time with a period of worship. Before beginning my Bible reading for the day, I take a few minutes to reflect upon one of the attributes of God or to meditate upon one of the passages about him mentioned above, and then ascribe to him the glory and honor due to him because of that particular attribute.

I find it helpful to assume a kneeling position for this time of worship as a physical acknowledgment of my reverence, awe, and adoration of God. Worship is a matter of the heart, not of one's physical position; nevertheless, the Scriptures do frequently portray bowing the knee as a sign of homage and adoration. David said, "in reverence will I bow down toward your holy temple" (Psalm 5:7). The writer of Psalm 95 says, "Come, let us bow down in worship, let us kneel before the Lord our Maker" (verse 6). And we know that one day every knee shall bow before Jesus as a sign of homage to his Lordship (Philippians 2:10).

Obviously, it is not always possible to bow before God in our times of worship. God understands this and surely allows for it. But when we can do so, I strongly recommend bowing before God, not only as a sign of reverence to him, but also for what it does in helping us prepare our minds to worship God in a manner acceptable to him.

In emphasizing the value of worship, I have dealt solely with the practice of private worship: that which we should do in our personal quiet time. I do not mean to ignore public, corporate worship; I simply do not feel qualified to speak on that subject. I would plead with ministers of congregations to give us more *instruction* in the nature and practice of corporate worship. I sense that many Christians go through the motions of a worship service without actually worshiping God.

Fellowship with God

All that has been said thus far about the importance of prayer, of meditating on the word of God, and of having a specific time of worship, implies the value of a quiet time. The expression "quiet time" is used to describe a regular period each day set aside to meet with God through his word and through prayer. One of the great privileges of a believer is to have fellowship with almighty God. We do this by listening to him speak to us from his word and by speaking to him through prayer.

There are various spiritual exercises we may want to accomplish during our quiet time, such as reading through the Bible in a year and praying over certain requests. But the primary objective of our quiet time should be fellowship with God—developing a personal relationship with him and growing in our devotion to him.

After I have begun my quiet time with a period of worship, I next turn to the Bible. As I read a passage of Scripture (usually one or more chapters), I talk to God about what I am reading, as I go along. I like to think of the quiet time as a conversation: God speaking to me through the Bible and I responding to what he says. This approach helps to make the quiet time what it is intended to be—a time of fellowship with God.

Having worshiped God and fellowshiped with him, I then take time to go over various prayer requests I want to bring before him that day. Following this order prepares me to pray more effectively. I have thought about who God is; therefore, I do not "rush into his presence" casually and demandingly. At the same time I am reminded of his power and love, and my faith regarding his ability and delight to answer my requests is strengthened. In this way, even my time of asking actually becomes a time of fellowship with him.

In suggesting certain Scriptures for meditation, or certain modes of worship, or a particular practice for a quiet time, I do not want to give the impression that growing in devotion to God is merely following a suggested routine. Neither do I want to suggest that what is helpful to me ought to be followed by others, or will even be helpful to others. All I want to do is demonstrate that growth in devotion to God, although a result of his ministry in us, comes as a result of very concrete practice on our part. We are to train ourselves to be godly; and as we learned in chapter three, training involves practice—the day-after-day exercise that enables us to become proficient.

The ultimate test

Thus far we have looked at specific activities that help us grow in our devotion to God—prayer, meditation on the Scriptures, worship, and the quiet time. There is still another area that is not an activity, but an attitude of life: obedience to the will of God. This is the ultimate test of our fear of God and the only true response to his love for us. God specifically states that we fear him by keeping all his decrees and commands (Deuteronomy 6:1-2), and Proverbs 8:13 tells us that "To fear the Lord is to hate evil." I can know if I truly fear God by determining if I have a genuine hatred of evil and an earnest desire to obey his commands.

In the days of Nehemiah, the Jewish nobles and officials were disobeying God's law by exacting usury from their countrymen. When Nehemiah confronted them he said, "What you are doing is not right. Shouldn't you walk in the fear of our God to avoid the reproach of our Gentile enemies?" (Nehemiah 5:9). He could just as well have said, "Shouldn't you *obey* God to avoid the reproach of our enemies?" Nehemiah equated walking in the fear of God with obedience to God. If we do not fear God, we will not think it worthwhile to obey his commands; but if we truly fear him—if we hold him in reverence and awe—we will obey him. The measure of our obedience is an exact measure of our reverence for him.

Similarly, as we have already seen in chapter two, Paul affirmed that his awareness of Christ's love for him compelled him to live, not for himself, but for him who died for us. As God begins to answer our prayer for a deeper realization of his love, one means he often uses is to enable us to see more and more of our own sinfulness. Paul was nearing the end of his life when he wrote these words: "Christ Jesus came into the world to save sinners—of whom I am the worst" (1 Timothy 1:15). We realize that our sins as Christians, though perhaps not as outwardly gross as before, are more heinous in the sight of God because they are sins against knowledge and against grace. We know better and we know his love, and yet we sin willfully. And then we go back to the cross and realize that Jesus bore even those willful sins in his body on the tree, and the realization of that infinite love compels us to deal with those very sins and to put them to death. Both the fear of God and the love of God motivate us to obedience, and that obedience proves they are authentic in our lives.

A deeper longing

As we concentrate on growing in our reverence and awe for God and in our understanding of his love for us, we will find that our desire for him will grow. As we gaze upon his beauty we will desire to seek him even more And as we become progressively more aware of his redeeming love, we will want to know him in a progressively deeper way. But we can also pray that God will deepen our desire for him. I recall reading Philippians 3:10 a number of years ago and realizing a little bit of the depth of Paul's desire to know Christ more intimately. As I read I prayed, "O God, I cannot identify with Paul's longing, but I would like to." Over the years God has begun to answer that prayer. By his grace I know experientially to some degree Isaiah's words, "My soul yearns for you in the night; in the morning my spirit longs for you" (Isaiah 26:9). I am grateful for what God has done, but I pray I will continue to grow in this desire for him.

One of the wonderful things about God is that he is infinite in all of his glorious attributes, so never in our desire for him will we exhaust the revelation of his person to us. The more we come to know him, the more we will desire him. And the more we desire him, the more we will want to fellowship with him and experience his presence. And the more we desire him and his fellowship, the more we will desire to be like him.

Paul's heartfelt cry in Philippians 3:10 vividly expresses this longing. He desires both to know Christ and to be like him. He wants to experience both his fellowship—even the fellowship of suffering—as well as the transforming power of his resurrection life. He wants both Christ-centeredness and Christ-likeness.

This is godliness: God-centeredness, or devotion to God; and Godlikeness, or Christian character. The practice of godliness is both the practice of devotion to God and the practice of a lifestyle that is pleasing to God and that reflects his character to other people.

In the remainder of our studies in this book we will consider the Godlike character that we should display. But we can build Godlike character only upon the foundation of a wholehearted devotion to God. God must be the very focal point of our lives if we wish to have godly character and conduct.

This point cannot be overemphasized. Too many of us focus on the outward structure of character and conduct without taking the time to build the inward foundation of devotion to God. This often results in a cold morality or legalism, or even worse, self-righteousness and spiritual pride. Of course, the foundation of devotion to God and the structure of a life pleasing to God must be developed simultaneously. We cannot separate these two aspects of godliness.

Because of the importance of properly laying the foundation of inward devotion, I encourage you to review the essential elements of devotion (see chapter two). Then review this chapter and make specific plans for exercising yourself in the area of devotion to God. No one has ever developed a mental or physical skill without a commitment to practice. And no one will ever develop a devotion to God without a commitment to exercise himself in the essential elements of devotion.

The idea of practice may tend to make us think of drudgery, such as dreary drills on piano scales when we wished to be out playing with our friends. But the practice of developing our relationship with God should not be equated with something like childhood music lessons. We are seeking to grow in our devotion to the most wonderful Person in all of the universe, the infinitely glorious and loving God. Nothing can compare with the privilege of knowing him in whose presence is fullness of joy and in whose hand there are pleasures forever (Psalm 16:11, *New American Standard Bible*).

5
Taking on God's Character

THEREFORE, AS GOD'S CHOSEN
PEOPLE, HOLY AND DEARLY
LOVED, CLOTHE YOURSELVES
WITH COMPASSION, KINDNESS,
HUMILITY, GENTLENESS AND
PATIENCE.

Colossians 3:12

Godliness consists of two distinct but complementary traits, and the person who wants to train himself to be godly must pursue both with equal vigor. The first trait is God-centeredness, which we call devotion to God; the second is Godlikeness, which we call Christian character. Godly character flows out of devotion to God and practically confirms the reality of that devotion.

We may express a reverence for God; we may lift our hearts in worship to him; but we demonstrate the genuineness of our devotion to God by our earnest desire and sincere effort to be like him. Paul not only wanted to know Christ, he wanted to be like him; and he pressed forward with utmost intensity toward that goal.

Thus far in our study of the practice of godliness we have concentrated on the aspect of devotion, of God-centeredness. Now we turn our attention to Godlikeness—the development of Godlike character. What are the character traits that distinguish the godly person? A good place to start is with the list of gracious qualities, which Paul calls the fruit of the Spirit, in Galatians 5:22-23. It seems obvious, however, that Paul did not intend to limit the traits of the fruit of the Spirit to that particular list. Any other trait commended in Scripture as befitting a believer is also a fruit of the Spirit, since its evidence is a result only of the Spirit's ministry in our hearts. So, to the qualities listed in Galatians 5—love, joy, peace, patience, kindness, goodness, faithfulness, gentleness, and self-control—we can also add such traits as holiness, humility, compassion, forbearance, contentment, thankfulness, considerateness, sincerity, and perseverance.

This is a rather awesome list of character traits to pursue, and our first reaction, if we are realistic at all, is probably to say, "I can't work on all of these." That is indeed true, *if* we were left to our own devices. But these traits are the fruit of the Spirit, the result of *his* work within us. This does not mean we bear no responsibility for the development of Christian character, but rather that we fulfill our responsibility under his direction and by his enablement. It is this divine dimension that makes Christian character possible, and it is *only* this divine dimension that can keep us from becoming frustrated and defeated in our desire to exemplify godly character traits in our lives.

In the following chapters we will study some of these traits of godliness individually. There are some basic principles, however, that apply to all aspects of godly character.

The right motive

The first principle of godly character is, *Devotion to God is the only acceptable motive for actions that are pleasing to God*. This devotion may express itself in one of several different ways. We may have a sincere desire to please God or to glorify him; we may do or not do a particular action because we love God, or because we sense that he is worthy of our obedience. However our motivation expresses itself, if it is God-centered, it arises out of our devotion to God and is acceptable to him.

Unfortunately, too often our motives are self-centered rather than God-centered. We want to maintain our reputation before others, or we want to feel good about ourselves. Or we may even seek to live a decent and moral life or to do good deeds because such an ethic has been instilled in us from childhood. But that motivation is never related to God and thus is not acceptable to him.

When Joseph was enticed by Potiphar's wife, he did not refuse her on the basis, "If I did that and my master found out, he would have my head." No; he said, "How then could I do such a wicked thing and sin against God?" (Genesis 39:9). His motivation for morality was centered in God, and because of that it was acceptable to God.

I recall once being tempted with the opportunity to engage in a questionable business transaction, one of those gray-area situations in which we tend to rationalize our actions. As I pondered the matter I thought, I better not; I might incur the discipline of God. Now when all proper motives fail, it is certainly better to be checked by the fear of God's discipline than to go ahead with our sin. But that is not the right motive. In this situation the Holy Spirit came to my aid and I thought to myself, Now that [the fear of God's discipline] is certainly an unworthy motive; the real reason why I should not do that is because God is worthy of my most honorable conduct. The Holy Spirit helped me to recognize the self-centeredness of my initial motivation and to correctly focus my motivation on God.

When God commanded Abraham to offer up Isaac as a sacrifice, he tested his motive. As he stayed Abraham's knife from the fatal plunge, God said, "Now I know that you fear God, because you have not withheld from me your son, your only son" (Genesis 22:12). It was Abraham's fear of God that motivated him to go forward with that supreme act of obedience. We usually associate Abraham's obedience with his faith. It was by faith that Abraham was *enabled* to offer Isaac as a sacrifice, but it was the fear of God that *motivated* him. And it was this Godward motivation that the Lord saw and accepted and commended.

As we look into the New Testament we see this Godward motivation emphasized again and again. Jesus taught that all the Law and the Prophets hang on the two commandments of love for God and love for our neighbor (Matthew 22:37-40). He was not teaching merely that these two commandments of

love sum up all the other more specific commandments, but rather that all the other commandments
depend upon the motivation of love for their fulfillment. The fear of consequences may keep us from
committing the outward acts of murder or adultery,
but only love will keep us from committing murder or
adultery in our hearts.

In 1 Corinthians 10:31 Paul tells us that even our
eating and drinking is to be done for the glory of God.
As someone has observed, there is nothing more ordinary and routine than our eating and drinking; yet
even this is to be done with a Godward motivation.
Slaves were enjoined to obey their earthly masters out
of "reverence for the Lord" (Colossians 3:22). All of
us are to submit ourselves to human authority "for
the Lord's sake" (1 Peter 2:13). And our interper-
sonal relationships—our mutual submission to one
another—is to be done "out of reverence for Christ"
(Ephesians 5:21). All of our actions, to be acceptable
to God, must be done out of a sense of devotion to
God.

The source of power

The second principle of godly character is, *The power
or enablement for a godly life comes from the risen
Christ*. Paul said in relation to his ministry, "our
competence comes from God" (2 Corinthians 3:5),
and "I labor, struggling with all his energy, which so
powerfully works in me" (Colossians 1:29). He said of
his ability to be content in any situation, "I can do
everything through him who gives me strength"
(Philippians 4:13).

It is very likely that God, in his sovereign calling

and preparation of Paul for his tremendous task, had endowed him with more noble qualities and strength of character than any person since; yet Paul consistently attributes his spiritual strength and accomplishments to the Lord's power. I once heard someone say, "When I do something wrong, I have to take the blame, but when I do something right, God gets the credit." This person was complaining, but he was exactly correct. Certainly God cannot be blamed for our sins, but only he can provide the spiritual power to enable us to live godly lives.

As the *source* of power for godliness is Christ, so the *means* of experiencing that power is through our relationship with him. This truth is Jesus' essential teaching in his illustration in John 15 of the vine and the branches. It is only by abiding in him that we can bring forth the fruit of godly character.[1] The most helpful explanation I have found of what it means to abide in Christ comes from the nineteenth-century Swiss theologian Frederic Louis Godet: " 'To abide in me' expresses the continual act by which the Christian sets aside everything which he might derive from his own wisdom, strength, merit, to draw all from Christ."[2]

Paul expresses this relationship as "living in Christ." He says in Colossians 2:6-7, "So then, just as you received Christ Jesus as Lord, continue to live in him, rooted and built up in him, strengthened in the faith." The context of this statement is that all the wisdom and power for living the Christian life are to be found in Christ rather than in manmade philosophies and moralisms (see verses 2-4 and 8-10). This is what Godet is saying. We have to set aside any dependence upon our own wisdom and strength of character and draw all that we need from Christ through faith in him. This faith, of course, is expressed concretely by prayer to him. Psalm 119:33-37 is a good example of such a prayer of dependence.

This relationship is also maintained by beholding the glory of Christ in his word. In 2 Corinthians 3:18 Paul tells us that as we behold the Lord's glory, we are transformed more and more into his image. Beholding the Lord's glory in his word is more than observing his humanity in the gospels. It is observing his character, his attributes, and his will in every page of Scripture. And as we observe him, as we maintain this relationship with him through his word, we are transformed more and more into his likeness; we are enabled by the Holy Spirit to progressively manifest the graces of godly character.

So it is this relationship with Christ, expressed by beholding him in his word and depending upon him in prayer, that enables us to draw from him the power essential for a godly life. The Christian is not like an automobile with a self-contained power source; rather, he is like an electric motor that must be constantly connected to an outside current for its power. Our source of power is in the risen Christ, and we stay connected to him by beholding him in his word and depending on him in prayer.

Responsibility and dependence

The third principle of godly character is, *Though the power for godly character comes from Christ, the responsibility for developing and displaying that character is ours*. This principle seems to be one of the most difficult for us to understand and apply. One day we sense our personal responsibility and seek to live a godly life by the strength of our own willpower. The next day, realizing the futility of trusting in ourselves, we turn it all over to Christ and abdicate our responsibility which is set forth in the Scriptures. We need to learn that the Bible teaches both total responsibility and total dependence in all aspects of the Christian life.

I once read a statement to the effect that there is nothing a Christian can do to develop the fruit of the Spirit in his life; it is all the work of the Holy Spirit. Sensing that at best, such a statement failed to present a balance of scriptural truth, I took out my concordance and looked up various passages that referred to one or more of the nine character traits listed as fruit of the Spirit in Galatians 5. For every one of those traits I found one or more passages in which we are commanded to exhibit them. We are enjoined to love, to rejoice, to live in peace with each other, and so forth. These commands address our responsibility.

We have already seen that Timothy was responsible to train himself in godliness; he was to *pursue* godliness. When Paul describes his own pursuit of a Godlike life, he uses strong verbs such as ''press on'' and ''straining toward'' (Philippians 3:12-14). These words convey the idea of intense effort on his part and communicate forcefully his own sense of personal responsibility.

The solution to the seemingly incompatible statements that we are both totally responsible and totally dependent is found in Philippians 2:12-13: ''Therefore, my dear friends, as you have always obeyed—not only in my presence, but now much more in my absence—continue to work out your salvation with fear and trembling, for it is God who works in you to will and to act according to his good purpose."

Commenting on this passage, Professor Jac J. Müller says, "The believer is called to self-activity, to the active pursuit of the will of God, to the promotion of the spiritual life in himself, to the realization of the virtues of the Christian life, and to a personal application of salvation."[3] If we stopped at this point, it would appear that we are left to our own devices, to our own strength of character and our own willpower. But Paul does not stop with our responsibility. He says, "for it is God who works in you." The spiritual power that enables us to apply ourselves to the cultivation of Christian graces is of God, who works in us to will and to act.

Nineteenth-century Dutch Reformed pastor George W. Bethune put it this way:

> While, therefore, we grow in the Christian life by divine grace, it is *our duty* to grow in grace. Besides, the quality of grace is such that, though it is strength from God, we must use it. Grace gives no new faculty, but strengthens the faculties which we have. . . . Hence the fruits of the Spirit are the qualities and actions of the renewed man, not produced without him, but wrought through him. . . . Let us then be ever mindful of our entire dependence upon the Spirit of God . . . [but] let us be ever mindful of our duty "to maintain good works."[4]

Put off and put on

The fourth principle of godly character is, *The development of godly character entails both putting off and putting on character traits*. Paul says, "You were taught, with regard to your former way of life, to *put off your old self*, which is being corrupted by its deceitful desires; to be made new in the attitude of your minds; and to *put on the new self*, created to be like God in true righteousness and holiness" (Ephesians 4:22-24).

In the succeeding verses (4:28—5:4) Paul makes some very specific applications of this principle. We are to put off falsehood and put on truthfulness. We are to put off stealing and put on generosity. Unwholesome talk must be put off and replaced with speech which is helpful for building others up. Bitterness, rage, anger, and slander are to be replaced with kindness, compassion, and forgiveness. Obscene or suggestive speech is to be replaced with thanksgiving. Even Paul's list of gracious qualities in Galatians 5, called the fruit of the Spirit, is set in contrast to a lengthy catalog of vices of the sinful nature which must be put off by the godly person.

It was said of the Lord Jesus that he has both loved righteousness and hated wickedness (Hebrews 1:9). And we are to follow his example, for Paul instructs us to "hate what is evil; cling to what is good" (Romans 12:9). Surely we must put to death, by the aid of the Holy Spirit, the misdeeds of the body. But we must also, again with his enablement, clothe ourselves with compassion, kindness, humility, gentleness, and patience.

Just as we need to learn Scripture's teaching for

the dual principle of personal responsibility and total dependence, here also we need to seek the balance of Scripture in putting off and putting on. Some Christians have a tendency to emphasize only putting off traits of the sinful nature. They are usually very morally upright, but lacking in those gracious qualities of love, joy, and compassion. When a fellow Christian falls into sin, they do not seek to restore him gently, but rather ostracize him from their fellowship. A repentant Christian once wrote me that his church knew how to reach out to lost sinners but did not know how to restore one of its own errant members. This is the attitude we tend to develop when we put our entire emphasis in Christian character growth on putting off sinful habits.

But there is equal danger if we focus all our attention on such qualities as love and compassion while neglecting to deal with the vices of the sinful nature. Today, there is a good deal of emphasis on affirming and encouraging one another. We are to help one another "feel good about ourselves." We undoubtedly need such encouragement in the body of Christ, but we must not neglect the equally scriptural emphasis of putting to death the deeds of the sinful nature.

We are to put off the traits of the old self and put on the traits of the new. If we desire to be godly we must not neglect either of these biblical emphases.

Balanced growth
The fifth principle of godly character is, *We are to pursue growth in all of the graces that are considered the fruit of the Spirit*. This would include traits such

as compassion, forbearance, and humility that are not included in the nine-trait list of Galatians 5 but are obviously a result of his ministry in our lives. Godly character is balanced. It displays with equal emphasis the entire spectrum of graces that are set forth in the Scriptures as characteristic of the godly person.

We tend to emphasize in our lives those traits that seem most natural to our particular temperaments. But the fruit of the Spirit is not a matter of temperament; it is the result of the individual Christian seeking to grow, under the direction and aid of the Spirit, in every area of Christian character.

Author Tim LaHaye tells us that it was Hippocrates, the Greek physician and philosopher, who gave us the fourfold classification of temperaments so widely used today. He identified the jovial sanguine, the strong-willed choleric, the sensitive melancholic, and the dependable phlegmatic.

The sanguine person easily responds to the admonition to rejoice in the Lord or to be compassionate and tenderhearted. At the same time, he finds it difficult to exercise self-control or to be faithful with responsibilities. He must pray more earnestly and strive more diligently for these latter graces. Above all, he must be convinced of the necessity in his life of those graces that are most difficult to display. He must not excuse himself for his lack of faithfulness on the basis of, "That's just the way I am."

Similarly, the even-tempered, often unemotional phlegmatic person easily responds to the need for faithfulness but may have difficulty with the fruit of joy. I personally identify with this type of person. Faithfulness is very high in my value system; when given a responsibility, I am usually conscientious about fulfilling it. But I have to give special attention to joy. A number of years ago, God brought to my attention that "the kingdom of God is not a matter of eating and drinking, but of righteousness, peace and joy in the Holy Spirit" (Romans 14:17). I realized that joy in the Lord was just as important as any other trait of godly character.

Futhermore, even those traits to which we most naturally respond need to be developed under the ministry of the Spirit. God has a way of putting us in situations that exercise our character in those areas in which we feel we are strong, in order that the fruit might be of the Spirit, not of ourselves. For example, the naturally faithful person might stop short of dependability if it becomes inconvenient. But the godly person keeps his word even when it is costly.

The choleric individual can't understand why anyone else has difficulty with self-control. He is usually so self-disciplined that this trait of godly character seems to come naturally to him. But as a godly person seeking to display all the fruit of the Spirit, he may weep over his lack of patience and gentleness in his relationships with others.

The melancholic person is usually sensitive to the needs of others and is often self-sacrificing in his relationships. At the same time, he has a tendency to be critical and unforgiving, so he needs to especially look to the Holy Spirit for his ministry in those areas of need.

I do not intend this section to be an amateur psychological analysis of various temperament types. Rather, I am seeking to demonstrate the varying needs each of us will have in displaying the fruit of the Spirit in our lives. The principle to learn and apply is, *We are responsible to exhibit all of the traits of godly character in a balanced fashion*. Some traits are more difficult to grow in than others. These will require extra prayer and attention on our part, but that is simply the price we must pay to grow in Godlikeness.

Growth is progressive

The sixth principle of godly character is, *Growth in all areas is progressive and never finished*. Even the apostle Paul recognized this truth in his own life. In the context of his great longing to know Christ and to be like him, he said, "Not that I have already obtained all this, or have already been made perfect, but I press on . . ." (Philippians 3:12). In prison, near the end of his apostolic career, he was still pressing on, exerting every effort to continue growing in his knowledge and likeness of Christ.

Even in those areas in which we have grown, there is always need for further growth. Paul wrote in his first letter to the Thessalonian Christians that they had been taught by God to love one another and, in fact, they did love all the brothers throughout Macedonia. That is quite a commendation! But Paul was not satisfied. He went on to say, "Yet we urge you, brothers, to do so more and more" (4:9-10). Growth in Christian character is never finished until we go to be with Christ and are transformed completely into his likeness.

Growth in godly character is not only progressive and always unfinished, it is absolutely necessary for spiritual survival. If we are not growing in godly character, we are regressing; in the spiritual life we never stand still. The word *train* in Paul's admonition to Timothy, "Train yourself to be godly," occurs only four times in the New Testament: 1 Timothy 4:7, Hebrews 5:14 and 12:11, and 2 Peter 2:14. In three of those instances, the result of such training is positive and God-honoring.

But consider the fourth passage, 2 Peter 2:14. The context is Peter's sharp denunciation of and warning against false teachers. He refers to them as "experts in greed." The word *expert* is the same word translated in the other three passages as "train." In fact, the *New American Standard Bible* renders it, "having a heart trained in greed."

The implication of Peter's use of the word *train* is very sobering. It is possible to train ourselves in the wrong direction! That is what these false teachers had done. They had *practiced* greed so well that they had become experts in it—they had trained their hearts in greed!

So there is a sense in which we are growing in our character every day. The question is, In which direction are we growing? Are we growing toward godly character or ungodly character? Are we growing in love or selfishness; in harshness or patience; in greed or generosity; in honesty or dishonesty; in purity or impurity? Every day we are training ourselves in one direction or the other by the thoughts we think, the words we say, the actions we take, the deeds we do.

This sense of progression in character, in either one direction or the other, is also taught in Romans 6:19. Paul refers to the Roman Christians' former bondage to sin and to *ever-increasing wickedness*.

They were well on their way to becoming experts in wickedness. But now, says Paul, having been freed from the slavery of sin, they are to offer their bodies in slavery to righteousness *leading to holiness*. Righteousness refers here to obedience to God, specific "right actions." Holiness refers to the state or character resulting from those actions; right actions, or obedience, leads to holiness. Of course, both the actions and the character are the result of the working of the Holy Spirit, but he works as we work, and we are able to work because he is at work in us.

The relationship between conduct and character is an intimate one. In the form of repeated actions over time, conduct produces character. That is the teaching of 2 Peter 2:14 and Romans 6:19. But it is also true that character determines actions. What we do, we become. What we are, we do. This truth can be illustrated by a circle formed by two curved arrows feeding into each other.

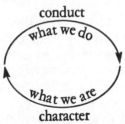

conduct

what we do

what we are

character

Conduct is always feeding character, but character is also always feeding conduct. Paul's experience while shipwrecked on the Island of Malta furnishes a good example of this relationship. The islanders built the refugees a fire because of the rain and cold. Luke relates in Acts 28 that Paul gathered a pile of brushwood, and, as he put it on the fire, a snake came out of the brushwood and fastened itself on Paul's hand. Under the adverse circumstances of shipwreck, why would Paul have gone about gathering fuel for a fire built and tended by someone else? Why didn't he just stand by the fire and warm himself? He didn't because it was his character to serve (see Acts 20:33-35 and 1 Thessalonians 2:7-9). He had learned well the lesson Jesus taught us when he washed his disciples' feet. Because it was Paul's character to serve, he gathered the brushwood instinctively. He probably did not even think about it. He just did what his servant character dictated at the moment.

Since conduct determines character, and character determines conduct, it is vitally important—extremely necessary—that we practice godliness every day. That is why Peter says, ''Make every effort to add to your faith . . . godliness'' (2 Peter 1:5-6). There can be no letup in our pursuit of godly character. Every day that we are not practicing godliness we are being conformed to the world of ungodliness around us. Granted, our practice of godliness is imperfect and falls far short of the biblical standard. Let us, nevertheless, press on to know Christ and to be like him.

Form reasonable expectations

There is a very important truth you should know and keep in mind as you pursue godliness. Otherwise, as you get into the following chapters on godly character, you may feel overwhelmed. As you study the twelve different traits of godly character, each one with several different potential applications, you could easily end up with a list of twenty or so areas of need in which you should grow in Christian character.

Don't fall into such a trap. It will cause you to diffuse your spiritual energies over much too broad an area. Your efforts would be general, scattered, and wasteful, and you would probably not make progress in any area of need. Then the devil would use that to discourage you.

The apostle Paul twice describes Christians as people who are *led* by the Holy Spirit (Romans 8:14 and Galatians 5:18). Both of these passages refer to his leading, not in some decision we must make, but in the conduct and character issues of our lives. If we are led by the Spirit, we will put to death the misdeeds of the body, and we will not gratify the desires of the sinful nature.

The Holy Spirit leads us *objectively* through the general teaching of his word. There is where we learn his will for all Christians. But the Holy Spirit also leads us *subjectively* as he impresses certain Scriptures on our minds, applying them to specific situations in our lives. This is his way of showing us what he wants us to give attention to at a particular time; this is the way he leads us to establish a priority of applications. And this is the important truth we must grasp hold of in our quest for godliness.

As you read the following chapters on godly character, take note of the general principles set forth. Seek to memorize at least one passage of Scripture on each character trait to store up the essence of the biblical teaching on that trait. These Scripture passages will then be available in your mind for the Holy Spirit's use in particular applications.

In addition to the general principles, ask the

Holy Spirit to impress upon your mind the two or three traits of godly character he wants you to work on and pray about now. Concentrate on these. Later on, the Spirit will lead you to work on others. Remember, he is in charge of our growth in godly character; he is our teacher and coach. And he will never lead us in a way that will overwhelm or confuse us.

Notes

1. I believe it is the fruit of godly character and conduct that is primarily in view in this passage (John 15:1-6). When Jesus and Paul speak of the fruit of evangelism, they speak of harvesting or gathering, as opposed to producing, fruit (John 4:36, Romans 1:13). Certainly Jesus' use of the term *fruit* in Matthew 7:15-23 relates primarily to character and conduct.
2. Frederic Louis Godet, *Commentary on John's Gospel* (Grand Rapids, Mich.: Kregel Publications, 1978), page 855.
3. Jac J. Müller, ''The Epistles of Paul to the Philippians and to Philemon,'' *The New International Commentary on the New Testament* (Grand Rapids, Mich.: Eerdmans, 1978), page 91.
4. George W. Bethune, *The Fruit of the Spirit* (1839; rpt. Swengel, Penn.: Reiner Publications), pages 32-34.

6
Humility

FOR EVERYONE WHO EXALTS
HIMSELF WILL BE HUMBLED, AND
HE WHO HUMBLES HIMSELF WILL
BE EXALTED.

Luke 18:14

Devotion to God is the first aspect of godliness; Godlike character is the second. There may be some question about whether or not humility is a Godlike quality, since humility is a trait befitting the creature, not the Creator. But there is no question that God commends humility and delights in it in his people.

Two passages from the book of Isaiah show us very clearly the esteem with which God views the humble person. We read in Isaiah 57:15,

> For this is what the high and lofty One says—
>   he who lives forever, whose name is holy:
> "I live in a high and holy place,
>   but also with him who is contrite and lowly
>   in spirit,

to revive the spirit of the lowly
and to revive the heart of the contrite.''

And then we read in Isaiah 66:1-2,

This is what the Lord says:
''Heaven is my throne
and the earth is my footstool.
Where is the house you will build for me?
Where will my resting place be?
Has not my hand made all these things,
and so they came into being?''

declares the Lord.

''This is the one I esteem:
he who is humble and contrite in spirit,
and trembles at my word.''

Not only does God commend humility in his people; our Lord displayed it in his humanity. ''And being found in appearance as a man, he humbled himself and became obedient to death—even death on a cross!'' (Philippians 2:8). Jesus Christ exemplified humility in its utmost through his death for us. But he also exemplified humility throughout his life. He was born in the very humblest of circumstances; he was obedient to his earthly parents; he called people to himself as one who was ''gentle and humble in heart''; he said, ''I am among you as one who serves''; he washed the disciples' feet on the very night of his betrayal; and he taught, ''he who humbles himself will be exalted.'' If we question whether humility is technically a *Godlike* trait (as we view God in his majesty), we certainly cannot question that it is a *Christlike* trait. And we are to be imitators of him as he lived out his human life on earth.

The promises of God toward the truly humble are almost breathtaking. The infinitely high and lofty One who lives forever promises to dwell with them, to esteem them, to give them grace, to lift them up, and to exalt them (see Isaiah 57:15 and 66:2, James 4:6, 1 Peter 5:6, and Luke 18:14). Humility opens the way to all other godly character traits. It is the soil in which the other traits of the fruit of the Spirit grow.

Humility manifests itself in our relationships—to God, to ourselves, to others. We are to be humble toward God and his word, humble in regard to trials and blessings that come our way or abilities and achievements with which we are blessed, and humble toward other people. Humility is the proper attitude with which to approach all these relationships and circumstances. Like love, it defies adequate definition; it can only be described and understood as it is applied to everyday living.

Humility before God

Humility toward God is akin to the fear of God: it begins with a high view of God's person. As we see God in his majesty, awesomeness, and holiness, we are humbled before him. In every occasion in the Scriptures in which man was privileged to view God in his glory, he was brought low or humbled in the presence of God. Moses bowed to the ground and worshiped; Isaiah cried, "Woe is me!"; Ezekiel fell face down; John fell at his feet as though dead. Even the four living creatures and the twenty-four elders in heaven of Revelation fell down before the throne of the glorified Lamb.

Humility in every area of life, in every relationship with other people, begins with a right concept of God as the One who is infinite and eternal in his majesty and holiness. We are to humble ourselves under God's mighty hand, approaching every relationship and every circumstance in reference to him. When relationships with people are good and circumstances are favorable, we are to humbly receive these blessings from his gracious hand. When people are mistreating us and circumstances are difficult, we are to humbly accept them as from an infinitely wise and loving heavenly Father.

This humility before God is basic to all our relationships in life. We cannot begin to experience humility in any other relationship until we experience a deep and profound humility in our attitude toward God. When we are conscious of our (sinful) creature relationship to an infinitely majestic and holy God, we will not wish to selfishly compare ourselves with others. And to the extent that our awareness of our lowly place before God is an abiding one, we will avoid the temptations of pride and competition.

Trembling at his word

The person who is truly humble before God is also humble before God's word. God says he esteems the person who is humble and contrite in spirit, and who trembles at his word. When King Josiah heard the words of the Book of the Law, he tore his robes, saying, "Great is the Lord's anger that burns against us because our fathers have not obeyed the words of this book . . .'' (2 Kings 22:11-13). Josiah realized that the word of God was the expression of the will of God, that it was to be obeyed, and that failure to obey would incur the judgment of God. Because Josiah trembled at the word of God, his heart was responsive, he humbled himself, he acknowledged the sin of his people, and God heard him. He did not dispute the word of God; he simply obeyed it.

We also must develop this kind of humility toward the Bible. As we search the Scriptures, we must allow them to search us, to sit in judgment upon our character and conduct. We must not treat the Scriptures only as a source of knowledge about God, but also as the expression of his will for our daily lives. As someone has said, ''The Bible was given not just to increase our knowledge, but to guide our conduct.'' Far too often it seems we approach the Bible just to increase our knowledge of the facts of the Bible. We do need to increase our spiritual knowledge, but it should be for the purpose of obeying God's will. Paul prayed that God would fill the Colossian Christians with the knowledge of his will in order that they might live a life worthy of the Lord and please him in every way. He wanted them to know God's will so that they would obey God's will and thus please God.

Not only must we develop a spirit of humility toward the Bible in regard to our *conduct*, we must also develop such a spirit in regard to our *doctrines*. We evangelicals are not noted for our humility about our doctrines—our beliefs about what the Bible teaches in various areas of theology. Whatever position we take in a specific area of theology, we tend to feel our position is airtight, and that anyone holding a different view is altogether wrong. We tend to be quite impatient with anyone who differs from us. Ironically, the more our views come from the teachings of someone else instead of from the Bible itself, the more rigidly we tend to hold those views.

It is one thing to be persuaded that what we believe is correct as we understand the Scriptures; it is quite another to believe that our views are *always* correct. Twice in my life I have had to make significant changes in my doctrines as a result of additional understanding of the Scriptures. This is not to suggest that we are to be wishy-washy in our beliefs so that we are "blown here and there by every wind of teaching," but that we are to hold our beliefs in a spirit of true humility We must remind ourselves that God has not seer fit to make our minds, or even a particular church, the depository of the sum total of his teaching.

At one time in his ministry Jesus prayed, "I praise you, Father, Lord of heaven and earth, because you have hidden these things from the wise and learned, and revealed them to little children. Yes, Father, for this was your good pleasure" (Luke 10:21). Commenting on this passage, Norvel Geldenhuys has aptly remarked,

> The contrast pointed by the Savior is not that between "educated" and "non-educated" but between those who imagine themselves to be wise and sensible—and those who live under the profound impression that by their own insight and their own reasonings they are utterly powerless to understand the truths of God and to accept them.[1]

May God help us to be humble enough toward the Scriptures to be found in that group that Jesus called, "little children."

Here by the grace of God

When a believer is truly humble before God and his word, he will also be humble about his own gifts, abilities, and attainments. He will realize and gratefully acknowledge that all that he is and all that he has comes from the hand of God.

This aspect of humility actually begins with our understanding of personal salvation. All evangelicals agree that we are saved solely by the grace of God, apart from any works of our own. But do we believe, even in some undefined way, that we did contribute something to our salvation, something that implies that we were a little bit wiser, or a little smarter, or a little more responsive to God than others?

Some time ago I read a statement in which the writer said he realized that the only difference between himself and another group of people was that perhaps he had a little more reliance upon the grace of God. I am sure the writer meant this as an expression of humility, but it left me uncomfortable. Somehow I cannot imagine the apostle Paul finding any distinguishing difference in himself, even a little more reliance upon the grace of God. Instead I find him saying, "Christ Jesus came into the world to save sinners—of whom I am the worst" (1 Timothy 1:15). Paul never compared himself favorably with the unbelievers around him. He was too overwhelmed with the fact that the grace of God was sufficient to reach even him.

Our attitude of humility in regard to our salvation should carry over to a recognition that any of our abilities and achievements are equally a result of God's grace. In his first epistle to the Corinthian Christians, Paul minces no words on this subject: "For who makes you different from anyone else? What do you have that you did not receive? And if you did receive it, why do you boast as though you did not?" (4:7). Every ability and every advantage we have comes from God and has been given to us as a stewardship to be used in serving him. For some time after I went into "full-time" Christian work and was living on a mere subsistence income, I often struggled with thoughts of how much money I could have been making if I had followed the profession I was trained for in college. Finally I began to realize that it was God who had given me the advantage of a good education, and that I was not doing him a favor by being in his service full-time. All that I had came from him and was to be used for his glory.

Paul refused to take the credit for his abilities or even his diligent labors. Again in his first letter to the Corinthians he declares, "But by the grace of God I am what I am, and his grace to me was not without effect. No, I worked harder than all of them—yet not I, but the grace of God that was with me" (15:10). This passage used to puzzle me. It seemed as if Paul was trying to be both humble and proud. How could anyone dare to state publicly that he had worked harder than all the other apostles? But then I realized that Paul was ascribing even his hard work to the grace of God. Sometimes we hear some tired Christian describing how hard he has worked in the service of God, teaching Sunday school for ten years straight, or sponsoring a difficult junior high youth group, or being one of the faithful few at Wednesday night prayer meeting. Perhaps we ourselves have been one of those tired Christians. If so, let's remember to credit our hard work and faithful labors strictly to the grace of God.

We should ascribe any attainments, whether secular or spiritual, to the grace of God. When Moses was giving final instructions to the children of Israel prior to entering the promised land, he specifically warned them against the pride that comes with taking credit for successes: "You may say to yourself, 'My power and the strength of my hands have produced this wealth for me.' But remember the Lord your God, for it is he who gives you the ability to produce wealth, and so confirms his covenant, which he swore to your forefathers, as it is today" (Deuteronomy 8:17-18). Paul was just as emphatic about spiritual success when he wrote, "So neither he who plants nor he who waters is anything, but only God, who makes things grow" (1 Corinthians 3:7). The prophet Isaiah succinctly expressed the attitude we are to have toward accomplishments when he said, "Lord . . . all that we have accomplished you have done for us" (26:12).

While writing this chapter I had occasion to express appreciation to a fellow church member for a job well done. I liked his simple, humble response: "It was the Lord who did it." Humility with regard to ourselves, then, consists in ascribing all that we are, all that we have, and all that we have accomplished to the God who gives us grace.

Submission, service, and honor

A believer who is humble before God will also be humble toward other people. One way this humility expresses itself is in mutual submission to one another. Paul instructs us, "Submit to one another out of reverence for Christ" (Ephesians 5:21). Peter likewise says, "Clothe yourselves with humility toward one another" (1 Peter 5:5), and James tells us that submissiveness is characteristic of the wisdom that comes from heaven (James 3:17). What does it mean to submit to one another? Does it mean always giving in to others' demands or opinions? Not at all. It means to submit to *instruction* as well as *correction* from other believers; to be teachable or to be humble enough to admit we have erred when another believer corrects us.

Apollos and Peter are beautiful examples of men who submitted themselves to other believers. Apollos submitted himself to others' instruction. Luke tells us that Apollos was a learned man, with a thorough knowledge of the Scriptures, who had been instructed in the way of the Lord, and who spoke with great fervor and taught about Jesus accurately. Apollos was obviously a gifted and capable man, and apparently a "full-time Christian worker," but he had one defect. His knowledge about Christ was accurate but incomplete; he knew only the baptism of John. When Priscilla and Aquila, a godly "lay" couple in the church at Ephesus, heard Apollos, they invited him to their home and explained the way of God more adequately (Acts 18:24-26). It is evident that Apollos received their instruction because shortly thereafter, when Apollos wanted to go on to minister to the churches in Achaia, the church at Ephesus not only encouraged him but also wrote a letter to the Achaian Christians telling them to welcome him.

What a commentary on the humility of Apollos! What a sermon by example on what it means to submit to one another! Apollos was a capable, gifted minister; yet he was not above receiving instruction from Priscilla and Aquila. (It is not too hard to imagine in passing with what gentleness and consideration Priscilla and Aquila must have instructed Apollos. That is the other side of submission to one another—but more about that when we get to the trait of gentleness in chapter fifteen.)

Peter provides us with an example of submitting to the correction of another believer. Paul records that when Peter came to Antioch, he found it necessary to rebuke Peter because of his hypocrisy in regard to the Gentile Christians. Not only was Paul's rebuke severe; it was done openly before the other believers. The Scriptures do not tell us what Peter's reaction was, but apparently Peter did not harbor any resentment toward Paul. In one of his own letters he later refers to Paul as "our dear brother" and speaks of Paul's letters as Scripture—that is, as part of the divinely inspired writings of the word of God (2 Peter 3:15-16). Peter had evidently accepted Paul's rebuke. He had humbly submitted himself to the correction of another believer, even though that believer was "younger in the Lord" than he.

There is no question that submission to the unsolicited teaching or correction of others is difficult for our naturally proud hearts. But the context of Paul's instruction on mutual submission in Ephesians 5 indicates it is one of the evidences of being filled with the Spirit. Humility is a fruit of the Spirit, the result of his ministry in our hearts. But this ministry does not occur without deliberate, conscious effort on our part. The Spirit does not make us humble; he enables us to humble ourselves in these difficult situations.

Although submission is probably the most difficult application of humility toward others, it is by no means the only one. A very common occasion for showing humility is through *serving one another*. In this area Jesus is our greatest teacher and pacesetter. The foremost example is his washing the disciples' feet on the night of his betrayal, but Jesus' whole life was one of serving others. He said he did not come to be served but to serve; he went around doing good for others. Jesus even seems to indicate that he will still be serving us in eternity (Luke 12:37), as incredible as that may seem.[2]

In addition to the example he set for us, Jesus also taught us by precept the importance of serving one another. He indicated that true greatness in the kingdom of God does not consist in position but in serving one another, and he promised blessing to those who followed his example in serving others.

This demonstration of humility in serving others also requires the grace of God. Peter tells us that those who serve ''should do it with the strength God provides, so that in all things God may be praised through Jesus Christ'' (1 Peter 4:11). We all know people, even unbelievers, who seem to be natural servants. They are always serving others one way or another. But God does not get the glory; they do. It is *their* reputation that is enhanced. But when we, natural servants or not, serve in dependence upon the grace of God with the strength he supplies, God is glorified.

Dependence upon the grace of God not only results in God being glorified; it also makes it possible for those of us who are not natural servants to practice this aspect of humility. His grace is sufficient for all of our needs, whatever they may be. We can, by his enablement, *learn* to serve one another.

A third way we demonstrate humility is by *honoring* one another. Paul says in Romans 12:10, "Honor one another above yourselves," and in Philippians 2:3, "consider others better than yourselves." We are to place the other person above ourselves in matters of position, concerns, or needs.

Jesus rebuked the Pharisees for seeking the places of honor at a feast, telling them to instead seek out the lowest place. We may condemn the childish self-seeking of the Pharisees, but how about our own attitude? Do we maneuver for first place in line, or for the best seats at public meetings? Do we frequently assert ourselves at the expense of others, or do we consider their interests as well as our own?

If we are to experience the blessings promised to the humble we must work out this humility in our daily relationships with others. We must learn to submit to one another, to serve one another, and to honor or prefer one another above ourselves. Remember: the Spirit does not make us humble, but he enables us to humble ourselves. We must *learn* humility, just as Paul learned contentment, but in our efforts we are assured of the same enabling power he experienced (see Philippians 4:11-13).

Practicing humility

Here are some practical suggestions for learning humility. Begin by renewing your mind. The best way to do this is to memorize one or more passages of Scripture, choosing those you believe address most directly your areas of greatest need.

As we memorize and then meditate on Scriptures in this way, the Holy Spirit transforms us inwardly, changing our values; for example, we may begin to place greater importance on putting others ahead of ourselves. The Holy Spirit will also use these Scriptures we have memorized to convict us in specific situations when we fail to live up to our new values.

Confess any prideful ways, as the Holy Spirit convicts you, and pray for sensitivity to see yourself as God does. Also pray for the Holy Spirit to change you inwardly.

Finally, take whatever specific steps are necessary in order to obey God's direction to humble yourself. We are to humble ourselves before God. The word *humble*, when used in this way, is an action verb. We are to *do* something. It may be a specific act of putting another first, such as in a supermarket check-out line or in an opportunity for a choice job position. It might even be as drastic as telling our friends we have taken the credit for success that rightfully belongs to God. Whatever the area of humility we need to work on, it is important that we do so in dependence upon him who is at work in us.

Notes
1. Norvel Geldenhuys, ''Commentary on the Gospel of Luke,'' *The New International Commentary on the*

New Testament (Grand Rapids, Mich.: Eerdmans, 1977), pages 306-307.

2. William Hendriksen comments on this passage, "What is promised here, therefore, is that our Lord, at his second coming will, in a manner consonant with his glory and majesty, 'wait on' his faithful servants!" in his "The Gospel of Luke," *New Testament Commentary* (Grand Rapids, Mich.: Baker Book House, 1978), page 677.

7
Contentment

BUT GODLINESS WITH
CONTENTMENT IS GREAT GAIN.

1 Timothy 6:6

Contentment is one of the most distinguishing traits of the godly person, because a godly person has his heart focused on God rather than on possessions or position or power. As William Hendriksen has observed so well, "The truly godly person is not interested in becoming rich. He possesses inner resources which furnish riches far beyond that which earth can offer."[1]

The words that are rendered as "content" or "contentment" in our English Bibles actually mean "sufficiency."[2] The same word translated "contentment" in 1 Timothy 6:6 is rendered "all that you need" or "all sufficiency" in 2 Corinthians 9:8. When God said to Paul, "my grace is sufficient for you" (2 Corinthians 12:9), he used the same word translated elsewhere as "be content" (see Luke 3:14, 1 Timothy 6:8, Hebrews 13:5).

The contented person experiences the sufficiency of God's *provision* for his needs and the sufficiency of God's *grace* for his circumstances. He believes God will indeed meet all his material needs and that he will work in all his circumstances for his good. That is why Paul could say, "godliness with contentment is great gain." The godly person has found what the greedy or envious or discontented person always searches for but never finds. He has found satisfaction and rest in his soul.

The idea of contentment in the Bible is most often associated with possessions or money, but there are other areas of life in which we need to be content. After possessions, probably the most common need is to learn contentment with our place in society or in the body of Christ. Still a third area that demands our practice of contentment is the providence of God in such varied circumstances as physical limitations and afflictions, privations, unpleasant neighbors or living situations, trials, and even persecutions. These circumstances often cause the natural man to murmur and complain and to question the goodness of God in his life.

The very first temptation in the history of mankind was the temptation to be discontent. God had provided for Adam and Eve far beyond all they needed. Genesis states, "God made all kinds of trees grow out of the ground—trees that were pleasing to the eye and good for food." God withheld only one tree from Adam and Eve as a test of their obedience to him. And Satan used that one tree to tempt Eve by sowing seeds of discontent in her heart. He questioned the goodness of God to Eve, and that is exactly what discontent is—*a questioning of the goodness of God*.

Satan tried the same strategy with Jesus in the wilderness. He sought to make Jesus discontent over his lack of food and covetous for position and power over the kingdoms of the world. If Isaiah 14:13-15 is a veiled reference to Satan, as many scholars believe, then we can conclude that Satan's own downfall was occasioned by his discontent—his unwillingness to accept his God-ordained position in the hierarchy of angelic beings.

We should note these incidents carefully. Discontent is one of the most satanic of all sins, and to indulge in it is to rebel against God just as Satan did.

Contentment with possessions

To be content with one's possessions is one of the most strongly worded exhortations in Scripture. God deemed it important enough to include a prohibition against covetousness together with prohibitions against the more abhorrent sins of murder, stealing, and adultery (Exodus 20:13-17). In his Sermon on the Mount, Jesus dwelt more extensively on the principle, "you cannot serve God and money," than on any other subject. While later addressing a dispute over an inheritance he said, "Watch out! Be on your guard against all kinds of greed; a man's life does not consist in the abundance of his possessions" (Luke 12:15). His double warning to us—"Watch out! Be on your guard"—alerts us to the extreme danger of being discontent with our possessions.

Paul has a similarly strong warning for us in his

first letter to Timothy as he urges us to be content with food and clothing, because the love of money is the root of all kinds of evil. He warns Timothy to "flee from" this love of money and discontentment with possessions (6:11). The writer of Hebrews frames his admonition in the form of encouragement as he urges us to keep our lives free from the love of money and be content with what we have, because God himself has promised never to leave or forsake us (13:5). So Scripture both warns us of the dangers of discontent and encourages us to pursue contentment on the basis of God's promise to provide for us.

In his letter to the Romans, Paul tells us that everything written in the past was written to teach us (15:4). The historical events recorded in the Old Testament, then, are not merely interesting anecdotes. They were written that we might learn from them. With this truth in mind, we need to give careful heed to the result of covetousness in the lives of Achan and Gehazi, as recorded in Joshua 7 and in 2 Kings 5. Achan's covetousness at the battle of Jericho resulted in the defeat of the army of Israel at Ai and his own untimely death by stoning. The covetousness of Elisha's servant Gehazi resulted in the affliction of the dread disease of leprosy on Gehazi and his descendants forever. In the New Testament, covetousness was the root of sin that brought down God's judgment upon Ananias and Sapphira (Acts 5:1-11).

It may be true that God's judgment upon covetousness and discontentment is not as severe or obvious in our day as it was in the days of Achan, Gehazi, and Ananias and Sapphira. Yet God's *attitude* toward discontentment has not changed, and the spiritual danger of loving the things of this world is far more serious than the judgment of a dreaded disease or an untimely death. John says very plainly that if anyone loves the world, the love of the Father is not in him. In other words, he is not a Christian! John makes it clear that a craving for possessions is being in love with the world.

In view of such strong biblical warnings against covetousness and the earnest exhortations of the New Testament writers to be content with what we have, we must take seriously the need to earnestly pursue contentment as a dominant character trait in our lives. It is not a spiritual luxury. Contentment with what we have is absolutely vital to our spiritual health.

How then can we pursue an attitude of being content with what we have? What are some practical steps we can take? As with every other character trait, begin renewing your mind by memorizing and meditating on one or two passages of Scripture you find especially helpful in this area. You may want to use Luke 12:15, 1 Timothy 6:6-8, or Hebrews 13:5, or perhaps some other passages from your own personal study. As you meditate on these verses, ask God to bring to your mind any specific areas in your life in which you are discontent with what you have. Decide on what definite steps you can and should take to deal with that area, and begin to take those steps.

Keep in mind, however, that only the Holy Spirit can work a lasting and fundamental attitude change deep in your heart, so make contentment a matter of regular, earnest prayer. I often pray as David did in Psalm 119:36-37, ''Turn my heart toward your statutes and *not toward selfish gain. Turn my eyes away from worthless things*; renew my life according to your word.''

Prayer and meditation on Scripture passages are essential to developing contentment about possessions. I've also found the following scriptural principles especially helpful in this area.

Our focus should be on the true values of life. In Mark 8, Jesus teaches that eternal life is more valuable than all the world. David declares in Psalm 19 that the word of God is more precious than gold. Solomon tells us that wisdom (an understanding and application of the moral principles of God) is more profitable than silver or gold or precious jewels (Proverbs 3:13-15). These statements all reflect God's value judgments about what is truly important in life. We have to decide whether we will accept them and make them our own values. To the extent we do, we are well on our way to experiencing contentment about possessions.

Service to God through service to mankind is the only motivation acceptable to God for diligence and hard work in our vocational calling. We must avoid selfish ambition (the desire for more money or prestige), and instead make it our ambition to please God in all of our work. We should, therefore, look at our job or our business not in terms of larger salaries, greater commissions, or increased sales, but in terms of how we may best please God. Vocational success should not be measured in terms of one's bank account or material possessions but in terms of service to others that is acceptable to God. Such an attitude, rather than fostering indifference to work, should promote greater diligence. Paul told the Colossians that slaves were more accountable to God for their work than they were to their earthly masters. This principle obviously applies to employment relationships of today.

All that we have comes from God as a result of his grace. As David so wisely acknowledged, "Wealth and honor come from you . . . in your hands are strength and power to exalt and give strength to all" (1 Chronicles 29:12). As in developing humility, we can learn contentment by remembering that it is God who gives anyone the ability to produce wealth (Deuteronomy 8:18). Humility toward God and contentment toward possessions, in fact, are handmaidens of each other. If I accept all I have now as a gift of God's grace and am thankful for it, I will not be secretly feeling that I deserve more and longing for greater possessions.

God in his sovereign good pleasure has seen fit to give some people more wealth and possessions than others; consequently we are not to envy them. In an effort to teach that all reward is of grace, Jesus told the parable of the workers in the vineyard. He described the situation of workers who labored for only the last hour of the day receiving the same pay as those who labored all day. Those who had worked all day became envious of the generous treatment accorded the workers who came later, and they began to grumble. But the master of the vineyard silenced them with the statement, "Don't I have a right to do what I want with my own money? Or are you envious because I am generous?" With this parable Jesus teaches us that God, who owns everything, has a right to dispense the material possessions of this world as he desires, and we are not to question him or envy the recipients of his favors.

For those whom God has blessed with wealth or an abundance of possessions, with privilege comes responsibility. "From everyone who has been given much, much will be demanded; and from the one who has been entrusted with much, much more will be asked" (Luke 12:48). Paul told Timothy to "Command those who are rich . . . to do good, to be rich in good deeds, and to be generous and willing to share" (1 Timothy 6:17-18).

This principle applies to most people who will read this book, because we are in fact wealthy in terms of the vast majority of the people of the world.

We'll find that contentment comes when we share what we have with others. It is in this context of sharing with those in need that Paul declared in 2 Corinthians 9 that God is able to make all grace abound to us, so that we will feel sufficient—or content—in every respect.

Some may feel that we should encourage one another toward a "simplified lifestyle," or one as unencumbered by material possessions as possible. This subject can easily degenerate into legalism, however, in which we begin judging one another by perhaps arbitrary standards of what is and is not acceptable in the way of material goods and possessions. Instead, we should concentrate on being content in all our circumstances, and on living lives that are pleasing to God. The result of this kind of focus will be that our lifestyles will be the kind that God wants us to live.

Contentment with position

Having to some degree won the battle of contentment regarding possessions, many Christians all too often fail in the battle of contentment regarding position in the body of Christ. Like Diotrephes of old we love to be first (3 John 9). And if we are not first, or at least prominent, either we envy those in positions of prominence, or else we adopt the attitude, ''I'm just a nobody. God can't use me.'' It was to guard against this type of thinking that led Paul to write to the Roman Christians, ''do not think of yourself more highly than you ought, but rather think of yourself with sober judgment, in accordance with the measure of faith that God has given you'' (12:3).

Paul recognized, and wanted the Christians at Rome to recognize, that God has placed each of us in the body of Christ as it pleased him. Our duty is not to decide what we want to be or to do, but to discover on the basis of our capabilities and gifts what God wants us to do and to be. Contentment lies not in being first, but in being faithful to fulfill the function God has called us to in the body of Christ.

The greatest single help to me in learning to be content about position is to come to terms with the fact that all positions in the church are given by the sovereign grace of God. Paul said, ''we have different gifts, according to the grace given to us'' (Romans 12:6). We have not only different gifts, but also different capacities for the use of those gifts. In the parable of the talents, one servant was given five talents, another two, and a third only one. The accountability was proportionate to the number of talents. The servant entrusted with only two talents who used them to get two more received the same commendation and reward as the servant entrusted with five talents who used them to get five more. Presumably, the servant entrusted with only one talent would have been similarly rewarded if he had been faithful to use it to get even one more, instead of burying it in the ground.

Whether we have several gifts or only one, whether our gifts put us in a position of prominence or keep us always behind the scenes, the important truth is that those gifts have been given to us by grace. We did not deserve them; we did not earn them; they were sovereignly bestowed upon us. I don't deserve to be where I am in the body of Christ, and the prominent person doesn't deserve to be where he is. We are each in our place by God's grace.

And God *is* sovereign in the bestowal of his grace. Paul again makes this very clear in the ninth chapter of Romans when he asks, "Does not the potter have the right to make out of the same lump of clay some pottery for noble purposes and some for common use?" Although Paul wasn't asking this question within the context of the bestowment of gifts, the principle still applies. God has the right to put each of us where he pleases. He not only has the right, he exercises it, as 1 Corinthians 12 shows us. "All these [gifts] are the work of one and the same Spirit, and he gives them to each one, just as he determines."

How does my acknowledgment of God's sovereign grace in placing each of us in the body of Christ help me to be content? First, I realize that I am where I am not by chance, nor by the favor or disfavor of other people, but by the decision of an all-wise and all-loving heavenly Father. And he has plans for me, plans to prosper and not to harm me, plans to give me hope and a future (Jeremiah 29:11).

Second, I realize I do not deserve to be where I am. However obscure a position it might be, I identify with Paul when he said, "although I am less than the least of all God's people, this grace was given to me: to preach to the Gentiles the unsearchable riches of Christ" (Ephesians 3:8). I may not be a missionary as Paul was, but whatever my position in the body, it was given to me by God's grace.

Third, I realize that each part of the body is indispensable. Paul says the body grows "as each part does its work" (Ephesians 4:16). I am important to God and I am important to the body. This is true of every single Christian in the world!

As I realize and accept these truths I find not only contentment, but excitement. Paul tells us in Ephesians 2:10 that God has prepared in advance good works for each of us to do. As we accept our place in the body of Christ and seek to do these good works, we do find the fulfillment and contentment of a life lived in accordance with the purpose of God.

Along with accepting our position in the body of Christ, we also need to learn to be content with our position in society—our vocational calling. Vocational calling usually determines status as well as wealth. And because of the world's preoccupation with status, we often face the temptation to be discontent with our position in society. Just as we are tempted to covet possessions, so we are tempted to covet position.

Here again we must go back to the sovereignty of

God in all of life. God ultimately rules in the natural realm, just as he does in the spiritual, even though this aspect of his sovereignty may not always be apparent to us.

It is God who has created some to be farmers, some physicians, some building tradesmen, some salesmen, some bus drivers, and some airline pilots. If God did not rule in this manner, even in the lives of unbelievers, the world would be a chaotic place in which to live. We would have an oversupply of workers in some vocations and a critical shortage in others. The vocational imbalances that God does allow to occur arise out of man's greed in constantly pursuing higher paying jobs and professions.

The principles of contentment with our position in the body of Christ will apply with equal force to our vocational position if we realize that our vocational calling is just as much a trust from God as is our spiritual responsibility.

In an excellent article on the Puritan work ethic, Leland Ryken said,

> The Puritans declared the sanctity of all honorable work. In so doing, they rejected a centuries-old division of callings into 'sacred' and 'secular'. . . . This Puritan rejection of the dichotomy between sacred and secular work has far-reaching implications. It judges every honorable job to be of intrinsic value, and integrates every vocation with a Christian's spiritual life. It makes every job consequential by regarding it as the arena for glorifying and obeying God and for expressing love (through service) to a neighbor.[3]

Not only are some jobs more prestigious than others; some are more challenging and exciting than others. What are we to do if God places us in a vocational responsibility that seems dull and unchallenging? We go right back to the principles of contentment in the body of Christ: I am where I am by God's sovereign but loving appointment; I do not deserve to be even here; and my job, however dull, is necessary to the ongoing of society. If I will look to him, God will give me the grace (in the sense of divine enablement) to be faithful and content in a dull and unchallenging situation.

Does this mean that contentment is incompatible with ambition, that we should never aspire to more responsible or challenging jobs? Not at all. Paul's counsel to the Christian slaves at Corinth provides a principle for us today: "Were you a slave when you were called? Don't let it trouble you—although if you can gain your freedom, do so" (1 Corinthians 7:21). Whatever your situation is, be content—don't let it trouble you. But if you have an opportunity to improve your position, do so (unless, of course, doing so would violate the will of God in some other respect).

Every Christian should pursue excellence of workmanship and service in whatever vocational calling he finds himself. But he should do so to please Christ and to glorify him, not for the sake of personal ambition. In many instances such faithful service *will* result in promotion, for even the unbelieving world respects and rewards excellence. But faithful service is not a guarantee to a better position. God is sovereign over our position in society, and he places us and keeps us where he wants us to be. As the Scripture says so eloquently, "no one from the east or the west or from the desert can exalt a man. But it is God who judges: He brings one down, he exalts another" (Psalm 75:6-7).

Paul's secret of contentment

A Christian may be winning the battle for contentment with regard to possessions and position and still lose the struggle for contentment with the providence of God in his life. We live in a sin-cursed world, where even creation itself is subjected to frustration (Romans 8:20). Christians are not immune from the frustrating, irritating, often overwhelming circumstances of life.

But as Christians we believe that all circumstances come to us, not by chance, but through the often unfathomable will of an all-wise, all-powerful, and all-loving heavenly Father. Because of this we refer to our circumstances as being under the providence of God, the word *providence* basically meaning God's care of and control over all the universe.[4] That the Bible teaches such care and control is affirmed over and over again in the Scriptures. For example, Psalm 33:10-11 says, "The Lord foils the plans of the nations; he thwarts the purposes of the peoples. But the plans of the Lord stand firm forever, the purposes of his heart through all generations."[5]

But God's providence does not always appear favorable toward his children. We are at a loss to understand many events and circumstances that appear to cast doubt on his wisdom and love. As God himself said through Isaiah, "For my thoughts are not your thoughts, neither are your ways my ways. . . .

As the heavens are higher than the earth, so are my ways higher than your ways and my thoughts than your thoughts'' (Isaiah 55:8-9).

Other circumstances, though perhaps not severe or tragic, can be perplexing and frustrating: we experience varying physical limitations, chronic illnesses, and nagging injuries. We are placed with an inconsiderate roommate or find ourselves next door to annoying neighbors. We live in a city that is too large and crowded, or in a remote community that is too dull and boring. The climate is too dry or too humid. There are a thousand and one such circumstances that can make us fretful and discontented.

To make matters worse, our unbelieving neighbors often appear to have no problems. With Asaph of old we look at them and say, ''this is what the wicked are like—always carefree, they increase in wealth. Surely in vain have I kept my heart pure; in vain have I washed my hands in innocence'' (Psalm 73:12-13).

With such situations as these surrounding us, how can we learn, as Paul did, ''to be content whatever the circumstances'' (Philippians 4:11)? ''I have learned the secret of being content,'' Paul said, ''in any and every situation.'' What ''secret'' had Paul learned?

The Bible never tells us, but perhaps 2 Corinthians 12 gives us the answer. That chapter records Paul's experience of being caught up into heaven and hearing inexpressible things that man is not permitted to tell. To keep Paul from becoming conceited over these surpassingly great revelations, there was given to him ''a thorn in the flesh,'' a messenger of Satan, to torment him. Three times Paul pleaded with the Lord to take away the thorn, but God said to him, "my grace is sufficient for you, for my power is made perfect in weakness." As we noted earlier, the Greek word translated "is sufficient" is the same word rendered elsewhere as "be content."

This must be the secret Paul had learned: *God's grace is sufficient*, whatever the circumstance. And because God's grace is sufficient, we can be content. But to experience contentment we must, as Paul did, *accept* that God's grace is in fact sufficient. By acceptance I mean not just theological assent to a truth, but an authentic faith in his grace in the face of trying circumstances.

Since early childhood I have suffered a vision impairment that is often frustrating, and a total hearing loss in one ear that is often embarrassing (as when people speak to me and I don't hear them, and thus appear to be ignoring them). But those are not my only physical problems. One day I stood before the bedroom mirror and named seven distinct things that were "wrong" with my body; things I had often fretted about and murmured over. That day I said, "Lord, I accept the fact that you made me the way I am, and that your grace is sufficient for all these limitations." I cannot say I have not fretted over these problems since then, but I can now say I know how to be content with them: by accepting that God's grace is sufficient. Although I do not always apply this wonderful fact, it is true and it is always available. The choice to accept it and experience contentment is mine. And the choice is yours in your particular circumstances.

In all of the areas in which we are called upon to

be content—whether possessions, position, or the providence of God—the grace of God is the ultimate solution for our discontent. Grace, as used in the New Testament, expresses two complementary thoughts; God's unmerited favor to us through Christ, and God's divine assistance to us through the Holy Spirit. An understanding and appreciation of both of these meanings is necessary for us to be content. First, we must learn to live by the realization that whatever our situation might be, it is far better than we deserve. Actually, we deserve God's eternal judgment. It's been said, "Anything this side of hell is pure grace." This statement is true, and we must accept it and adjust our attitude accordingly.

Second, we must learn that however difficult and frustrating our circumstances might be, God's divine assistance through the Holy Spirit is available to help us to respond in a godly manner and to be content. When Paul said, "I can do everything through him who gives me strength," he was referring to God's divine enablement. He could have said, "I can do everything by his grace," and he would have been saying the same thing.

This is the secret of being content: to learn and accept that we live daily by God's unmerited favor given through Christ, and that we can respond to any and every situation by his divine enablement through the Holy Spirit.

Notes
1. William Hendriksen, *Commentary on I & II Timothy and Titus* (London: The Banner of Truth Trust, 1959), page 198.

2. W.E. Vine, *An Expository Dictionary of New Testament Words*, pages 226 and 1105.

3. Leland Ryken, "Puritan Work Ethic: The Dignity of Life's Labors," *Christianity Today*, 19 Oct. 1979, page 15.

4. Providence is defined theologically as "the unceasing activity of the Creator whereby, in overflowing bounty and goodwill, he upholds his creatures in ordered existence, guides and governs all events, circumstances, and free acts of angels and men, and directs everything to its appointed goal, for his own glory." *The New Bible Dictionary* (London: Inter-Varsity Fellowship, 1962; rpt Grand Rapids: Eerdmans, 1973), pages 1050-1051.

5. Other passages that affirm the truth of God's providence include Genesis 12:17, 20:6, and 50:20; Exodus 3:21, 8:22, and 9:29; Ezra 1:1; Proverbs 21:1; Daniel 4:34-35; Acts 16:6-7; and Romans 8:28.

8
Thankfulness

ENTER HIS GATES WITH
THANKSGIVING
AND HIS COURTS WITH PRAISE;
GIVE THANKS TO HIM AND PRAISE
HIS NAME.
FOR THE LORD IS GOOD AND HIS
LOVE ENDURES FOREVER;
HIS FAITHFULNESS CONTINUES
THROUGH ALL GENERATIONS.

Psalm 100:4-5

Some virtues of Christian character, such as holiness, love, and faithfulness, are godly traits because they *reflect* the character of God. They are Godlike qualities. Other virtues are godly traits because they *acknowledge and exalt* the character of God. They are God-centered qualities that enhance our devotion to God. Such are the virtues of humility, contentment, and thankfulness. In humility we acknowledge God's majesty, in contentment his grace, and in thankfulness his goodness.

Thankfulness to God is a recognition that God in his goodness and faithfulness has provided for us and cared for us, both physically and spiritually. It is a recognition that we are totally dependent upon him; that all that we are and have comes from God.

123

Honoring God

To fail to be thankful to God is a most grievous sin. When Paul recounts the tragic moral downfall of mankind in Romans 1, he begins with the statement, "although they knew God, they neither glorified him as God nor gave thanks to him, but their thinking became futile and their foolish hearts were darkened." To glorify God is to acknowledge the majesty and dignity of his person. To thank God is to acknowledge the bountifulness of his hand in providing and caring for us. And when mankind in their pride failed to give God the glory and thanks due him, God gave them up to ever-increasing immorality and wickedness. God's judgment came because man failed to honor him and to thank him. If failure to give thanks is such a grievous sin, then, it behooves us to cultivate a spirit of thankfulness that permeates our entire lives.

One of the most instructive passages on the subject of thankfulness is Luke 17:11-19, the account of the healing of the ten lepers. Here were ten men in the most pitiful of all human misery. Not only were they afflicted with a terrible and loathsome disease; they were outcasts from society because of their disease. They had no one to relieve either their physical or emotional suffering. And then Jesus healed them.

As these men went to show themselves to the priest and thus be restored to their families and friends, only one of them, realizing what had happened, turned back to give thanks to Jesus. Ten men were healed, but only one gave thanks. How prone we are to be like the other nine. We are anxious to receive but too careless to give thanks. We pray for God's intervention in our lives, then congratulate ourselves rather than God for the results. When one of the American lunar missions was in serious trouble some years ago, the American people were asked to pray for the safe return of the astronauts. When they were safely back on earth, credit was given to the technological achievements and skill of the American space industry. No thanks or credit was publicly given to God. This is not unusual. It is the natural tendency of mankind.

In addition to instructing us about human nature, the account of the ten lepers also instructs us about God. Thanking him for blessings we receive is very important to him. Jesus asked, "Were not all ten cleansed? Where are the other nine?" Jesus was very much aware that only one returned to give him thanks. And God is very much aware today when we fail to thank him for the ordinary as well as the unusual blessings that come to us daily from his hand.

Even the angelic beings around God's throne give him thanks. Revelation 4:9 speaks of their giving glory, honor, and thanks to him who sits on the throne and who lives forever. God has created both angels and men to glorify him and give him thanks. When we fail to do this we fail to fulfill one of his purposes for us.

Thanksgiving is taught in the Bible by both precept and example. In 1 Chronicles, the Levites who took part in the temple worship were to stand every morning to thank and praise the Lord. The Psalms contain some thirty-five references to giving thanks to God. In eighteen instances in his letters,

Paul expresses thanksgiving to God, and there are ten other instances in which he instructs us to give thanks. In all, there are approximately 140 references in the Bible to giving thanks to God. Thankfulness is no minor principle in God's sight. It is absolutely necessary to the practice of godliness.

One incident from the life of Daniel shows us the importance that this man of God put on giving thanks. We all know the story of Daniel in the lions' den, but do we remember how he got there? King Darius was persuaded by certain officials who were jealous of Daniel's position to issue a decree that for thirty days, anyone who prayed to any god or man other than King Darius would be thrown into the lions' den. When Daniel knew that the decree had been published, he went to his room and three times a day he got down on his knees and prayed, giving thanks to his God, just as he had done before.

Now if you and I prayed at *all* under those circumstances, we'd be pleading with God for his deliverance. No doubt Daniel did pray for deliverance; but he also gave thanks. Our situation is never so desperate that it is not fitting to give thanks to God. Paul teaches us this principle in Philippians 4:6 when he says, "Do not be anxious about anything, but in everything, by prayer and petition, *with thanksgiving*, present your requests to God."

When Paul wrote his letter to the Colossian Christians, he was seeking to deal with an infiltration of man-made philosophy and wisdom into their church. After declaring that all the treasures of wisdom and knowledge are hidden in Christ, he urges the Colossians, "So then, just as you received Christ

Jesus as Lord, continue to live in him, rooted and built up in him, strengthened in the faith as you were taught, and overflowing with thankfulness'' (2:6-7). Paul is dealing with the fundamental issues of the Christian life, and he includes the concept of thanksgiving as one of those fundamental issues. He says we are to *overflow* with thanksgiving. Thanksgiving is a normal result of a vital union with Christ, and a direct measure of the extent to which we are experiencing the reality of that union in our daily lives.

Purposes of thanksgiving

The primary purpose of giving thanks to God is to acknowledge his goodness and honor him. God says in Psalm 50:23, ''He who sacrifices thank offerings honors me.'' Psalm 106:1-2 says, ''Praise the Lord. Give thanks to the Lord, for he is good; his love endures forever. Who can proclaim the mighty acts of the Lord or fully declare his praise?'' When we give thanks to the Lord we proclaim his mighty acts; we acknowledge his goodness.

God is infinite in goodness to all his creatures. ''He causes his sun to rise on the evil and the good, and sends rain on the righteous and the unrighteous''; and ''he has compassion on all he has made'' (Matthew 5:45, Psalm 145:9).

He is most worthy of our praise and thanksgiving, especially if we are among his redeemed people, for he has blessed us not only in the temporal realm, but also with every spiritual blessing in the heavenly realms (Ephesians 1:3).

Thanksgiving promotes not only the glory of God, but also humility in us. It is the tendency of the sinful human heart—even the regenerated heart—to usurp the credit that rightfully belongs only to God. On several occasions God warned the children of Israel against this tendency (see Deuteronomy 8:11-14, 8:17-18, and 9:4-7). In David's prayer of thanksgiving for the gifts for the temple, he gratefully acknowledged that all of the abundance which the people brought came from and belonged to God. Paul constantly gave thanks to God for the spiritual progress of the churches under his care. He never took the credit for himself.

Thanksgiving also stimulates our faith. In Psalm 50:14-15, God connects thank offerings with calling upon him in the day of trouble. Remembering God's previous mercies encourages us to trust him for mercies we need today. Perhaps this idea is included in Paul's cure for anxiety in Philippians 4:6-7.

Finally, thanksgiving promotes contentment. Few things will stir up discontent within us as will our inner spiritual struggle between the sinful nature and the Holy Spirit. Its intensity caused Paul to cry out, "What a wretched man I am!" But then he finds relief and contentment in thanksgiving to God for the deliverance promised to us through Jesus Christ (Romans 7:24-25). Thanksgiving will also promote contentment about possessions, position, and providence by focusing our thoughts on the blessings God has already given, forcing us to stop spending our time yearning for things we do not have. Contentment and thanksgiving strengthen each other.

Cultivating a thankful heart
The foundation of an attitude of thankfulness is a life lived in fellowship with Christ. As Colossians 2:6-7

suggests, thankfulness is the overflow of being rooted and built up in Christ. As we abide in him, as we see his power at work in us and through us, as we call upon him for our needs and experience his provision, our response will be thanksgiving. Like any other trait of godly character, thankfulness is a result of the Holy Spirit's ministry in our hearts. He gives us a thankful spirit, but he does this through our fellowship with Christ.

But though an attitude of thankfulness is the work of the Holy Spirit, it also comes as a result of personal effort on our part. We must cultivate the habit of always giving thanks for everything (Ephesians 5:20). One way we can do this is to expand our mealtime expression of thanks to include other blessings beyond the food before us. Another way is to begin and end the day with a time of thanksgiving. Psalm 92:1-2 says, "It is good to praise the Lord and make music to your name, O Most High, to proclaim your love in the morning and your faithfulness at night." As we arise in the morning we can thank God for his love, which is assured to us throughout the day. As we retire we can thank him for specific demonstrations of his faithfulness during the day.

Another practical help is to write down the prayer requests you make to God; then keep those answered requests on your list until you feel you have adequately thanked God for his answer. Along with my written prayer requests, I also keep a list of significant blessings for which I am always thankful. I try to go over this list two or three times a week to express my thanks to God for his goodness to me. My thanksgiving list includes the following items:

- my personal salvation
- opportunities I have for spiritual growth
- the availability of the Bible
- the instruction and fellowship of our church
- the abundance of helpful Christian books
- opportunities for ministry and service
- godly parents
- a godly wife
- children who know Christ and are growing in him
- health of our family
- political freedom
- material provision for family needs.

Your personal thanksgiving list may not include all the items on my list, but it will likely include others. The important thing is to make such a list, and then use it. Set aside a period of time when you do nothing but thank God for the blessings on that list, as well as blessings more passing in nature.

Thanksgiving should also be included as a regular part of our intercessory prayer time. Paul seemed to always do this. He makes frequent statements in his letters such as, "We always thank God, the Father of our Lord Jesus Christ, when we pray for you" (Colossians 1:3). Later in that letter he instructs the Colossians, "Devote yourselves to prayer, being watchful and thankful" (4:2). When we pray without giving thanks we impoverish our own souls and render our prayers ineffective.

Along with the practical steps for cultivating an attitude of thankfulness and a habit of giving thanks, we need to remember the place of the word of God and prayer in developing traits of godly character. An ungrateful heart (which all of ours are by nature) must be transformed by the renewal of the mind. This transformation is the work of the Holy Spirit as we fill our minds with the word of God. Again I encourage you to memorize key verses on thanksgiving, using some of the passages cited in this chapter or others of your choosing. As you meditate on these verses, ask God to give you a genuine attitude of thanksgiving so that you, too, may be found in the company of the one leper who returned to give God thanks.

9
Joy

FOR THE KINGDOM OF GOD IS
NOT A MATTER OF EATING AND
DRINKING, BUT OF
RIGHTEOUSNESS, PEACE AND JOY
IN THE HOLY SPIRIT.

Romans 14:17

For a number of years the virtue of joy was not very evident in my life nor very high in my value system. As far as Romans 14:17 was concerned, I considered myself a man of peace, and I felt I was seeking after the ethical righteousness that is referred to in that passage. But I really hadn't given much thought to the importance God places on the fruit of joy in our lives.

Then one day as I was reading through Romans 14, I realized that God was not satisfied with only righteousness and peace in our lives. Paul tells us very plainly that the kingdom of God is a matter of not only righteousness and peace, but also *joy*. Furthermore, I learned from verse 18 that without joy, my life was really not very pleasing to God.

133

The fact is, only Christians have a reason to be joyful, but it is also a fact that every Christian *should* be joyful.

True Christian joy is both a privilege and a duty. Jesus said, "I have come that they [his sheep] may have life, and have it to the full" (John 10:10). He has come that our lives might be full of joy. Twice in his talk to the disciples on the evening of his betrayal, Jesus referred to the joy that he desired for them to have. He has done all to make it possible for us to live joyful lives.

But we are not to sit around waiting for our circumstances to make us joyful. We are *commanded* to be joyful always (1 Thessalonians 5:16). We are to rejoice always (Philippians 4:4). Paul is quite emphatic about this: "I will say it again: Rejoice!" Like the other character traits we have examined, joy is not an option available only to those whose temperament is conducive to it. God intends that every one of his children exhibit the fruit of joy.

Just being joyful is not enough, however; we should continually be growing in joy. It is a contradiction for a Christian who professes to be a child of the one and only God—who created the universe and who governs it for his glory and the good of his people—to wear a gloomy countenance. As John W. Sanderson says, "It is practical atheism, for it ignores God and his attributes."[1]

Yet if we are honest, most of us must admit that life is so often anything *but* joyful. It often seems that at best life is dull, and at worst it is filled with anxiety, conflict, and tension. What is it that blocks joy in our lives?

Stumbling blocks

One of the most common hindrances to joy is *sin in our lives*, or sinful attitudes in our hearts. Christian joy is essentially the enjoyment of God, the fruit of communion with him. Sin obviously breaks that communion and the enjoyment of his presence. When David was confessing his sin of adultery with Bathsheba, he prayed, "Restore to me the *joy* of your salvation" (Psalm 51:12).

Psalm 32:3-4 vividly describes David's lack of joy as he agonized over his sin. When we are not experiencing joy, we should examine our hearts and our lives. Are we doing or have we done something that is displeasing to God that we need to confess and forsake? Or, as is often the case, are we holding on to some sinful attitude such as envy or resentment, or a critical and unforgiving spirit? The fruit of joy cannot exist when such attitudes have control of our hearts. All sin, be it in attitude or action, must be dealt with if we are to display the virtue of joy in our lives.

Another stumbling block to joy is *misplaced confidence*. Paul told the Philippian Christians to "rejoice in the Lord" (3:1). He then made it clear that the opposite of rejoicing in the Lord is to put confidence in the flesh—in our good works or religious attainment. For the believers of Paul's day it was Jewish legalism. For us today it might be our personal disciplines such as a regular quiet time, a consistent Scripture memory program, or faithfulness in witnessing to non-Christians. Whatever it is, if the source of our confidence is anything other than Jesus Christ and his grace, it is a false and oft-interrupted joy. As Sanderson says, "even success in the Lord's work is a broken reed if we lean on it for security."[2]

If we are to have consistent joy, our attitude must be that expressed in the words of the old hymn:

My hope is built on nothing less
  than Jesus' blood and righteousness;
I dare not trust the sweetest frame,
  but wholly lean on Jesus' name.

In Luke's account of Jesus' sending out the seventy-two to preach, he says that they returned with joy and said, "Lord, even the demons submit to us in your name." Jesus responded, "However, do not rejoice that the spirits submit to you, but rejoice that your names are written in heaven" (10:17-20). It appears that Jesus was not discouraging joy in the ministry, but cautioning against the ground of one's joy being in the *success* of a ministry. Success in ministry comes and goes, but our names are written in heaven forever. The circumstances of this life rise and fall, but the assurance of being with Christ one day never changes. It is in this fact that our joy must be grounded.

I have referred earlier to the book, *The Pursuit of Holiness*, which I was privileged to write several years ago. God has blessed the ministry of that book far beyond my expectations, and he has done it purely by his grace. I sometimes think I feel as the little boy must have who gave Jesus his five small barley loaves and two small fish, then watched in utter amazement as Jesus used them to feed five thousand people. Although I rejoice at what God has done through *The Pursuit of Holiness*, the fundamental ground for my joy should be not in a book and its ministry, but in the fact that my name is written in heaven.

Perhaps you don't feel you have too much to show for your life. You haven't written a book, or seen scores come to Christ through your witness, or done anything else that seems significant. But is your name written in heaven? If it is, you have as much reason to rejoice as the most well-known and successful Christian. Nothing you or I will ever do can possibly compare with having our names written in heaven. The most humble Christian as well as the most famous Christian stand together on that common ground.

A third area that can choke off joy in our lives is the *chastening or discipline* that God often administers to his children. Scripture says, "No discipline seems pleasant at the time, but painful" (Hebrews 12:11). Discipline is never a joyful experience; it is not meant to be, else it would not accomplish its intended results.

If we lose sight of its intended results, or feel we don't deserve it, discipline can lead to self-pity. John Sanderson again provides a helpful insight into the relationship between discipline and joy when he says,

> If we only knew how bad we are, we would welcome chastening because this is God's way of getting rid of sin and its habits. But chastening is resented because we cannot believe that we have done anything worthy of it.[3]

The secret of maintaining some semblance of joy in the midst of discipline is to remember that "the Lord disciplines those he loves," and that "later on, however, it [the discipline] produces a harvest of righteousness and peace for those who have been trained by it" (Hebrews 12:6 and 11).

Experiencing trials of faith is a fourth hindrance to joy. Trials differ from discipline in that their purpose is to exercise our faith, not deal with sin in our lives. In his infinite wisdom, God allows trials in order to develop perseverance in us and to cause us to fix our hopes on the glory that is yet to be revealed.

Trials can come in many forms—nagging health problems, financial reverses, criticism and rejection, outright persecution. Whatever form the trial takes and however severe it may be, it is intended to strengthen our character. I once read of a sign on the entrance to a gymnasium that said, "No pain, no gain." To the weight lifters entering that door, the message was plain. They knew they had to endure the agony of lifting more than their muscles could comfortably handle if they wanted to increase their strength. So it is with faith. Our faith and perseverance can grow only under the pain of trial.

Frequently, our reaction to trials is like Job's. At the beginning of his testing, he reacted positively with the statement, "The Lord gave and the Lord has taken away; may the name of the Lord be praised" (1:21). But as time wore on and the trials, aggravated by the false accusations of his friends, continued, Job's faith and patience gave out. He was finally reduced to saying, "It profits a man nothing when he tries to please God" (34:9). But though Job's faith wore out, God's faithfulness did not. He stayed with Job until Job had learned the lesson of God's sovereignty, and then he gave Job twice as much as he had before.

God's faithfulness should also be of comfort to us in times of trial. "Though he brings grief, he will show compassion, so great is his unfailing love" (Lamentations 3:32).

Stepping-stones

Before considering any of the practical steps we can take to cultivate a joyful spirit, we must remind ourselves that joy is a fruit of the Spirit, the effect of his ministry in our hearts. Paul said in his letter to the Romans, "May the God of hope fill you with all joy and peace as you trust in him, so that you may overflow with hope by the power of the Holy Spirit" (15:13). It is by the power of the Holy Spirit that we experience the joy of salvation and are enabled to rejoice even in the midst of trials.

The Holy Spirit uses his word to create joy in our hearts. Romans 15 contains an interesting connection between God and the Scriptures. Verse 4 of that chapter speaks of the endurance and encouragement that come from the Scriptures; verse 5 says God gives endurance and encouragement. That God gives endurance and encouragement through the Scriptures should not surprise us. God is the source; the Scriptures are the means. The same truth applies to joy. Verse 13 speaks of the God of hope filling us with joy and peace as we trust in him. How would we expect God to fill us with joy and hope? The reasonable answer is by means of the comfort of the Scriptures.

When I have experienced the Lord's discipline, the passage in Hebrews 12:6, "The Lord disciplines those he loves,'' has been a source of comfort and a means of restoring joy. When I was once experiencing what for me was a rather severe trial, Psalm 50:15 became a source of comfort: "and call upon me in the day of trouble; I will deliver you, and you will honor me.'' On another occasion when I thought my future looked bleak I was enabled to rejoice in the Lord through the assurance of Jeremiah 29:11, "'For I know the plans I have for you,' declares the Lord, 'plans to prosper you and not to harm you, plans to give you hope and a future.'''

These are the words the Holy Spirit will use to promote joy in our hearts. In order for him to use the Scriptures, however, they must be in our hearts through regular exposure to and meditation upon them. This is our responsibility and is one of the practical means we must pursue to exhibit the fruit of joy.

But does the word always minister to us in times of need? Are there not times when the Scriptures seem barren and lifeless and utterly powerless to arouse the spirit of joy in the face of difficult trials? Yes, there are those times, but we must remember that it is the Holy Spirit who comforts us and enables us to rejoice. His word is simply his instrument. He works when and how he pleases, so we must look to him with faith and patience to bring life to his word and apply it to our hearts.

I well remember a time when our family was struggling through a series of financial reverses. There was one thing after another: injuries, emergency hospital care, things breaking down at home, and frequent car repairs. The final straw was when the car broke down on a trip and we had to leave it for repairs at an unknown garage for four days. Assuming the worst, I lost all sense of joy in the Lord because I was focusing on circumstances rather than on him. But sometime during those four days, the Holy Spirit enabled me to rest on the promise of Romans 8:28: that God was in control and was at work in those circumstances for my good. Romans 8:28 is a passage I had known for years, but it did not help until the Holy Spirit applied it to my heart and enabled me to believe it.

So again we see the principle set forth in chapter five—we are both responsible and dependent. I was responsible to exhibit the fruit of joy during that time of financial reversal, but I was absolutely dependent upon the Holy Spirit for the power to do it. As we look to him, though, let us remember that the purpose of rejoicing is not so we can feel better emotionally (though that will happen). The purpose of joy is to glorify God by demonstrating to an unbelieving world that our loving and faithful heavenly Father cares for us and provides for us all that we need.

Now for some specific practical aids to joy in our lives: an obvious one is, *Confess and forsake sin.* I have already referred to the lack of joy, or the strong spirit of oppression, that David experienced when he failed to deal with his sin (Psalm 32:3-4). But as David confessed his sin there was an interesting progression in his thoughts, starting from freedom from guilt, to faith in God's deliverance, to testimony to God's unfailing love, to rejoicing and singing (see verses 5-11).

God's forgiveness is always a source of amazement to me. It seems incredible that in spite of repeated sins, if we confess them, he is faithful and just to forgive them. And the continued faithfulness of God to forgive and to restore me to his fellowship is a source of joy to me. I am ready to sing just as David did.

A second specific aid to joy is, *Trust in God*. Romans 15:13 speaks of God filling us with joy and peace as we trust in him. It is God who stands behind his word. The promises of the Bible are nothing more than God's covenant to be faithful to his people. It is his character that makes these promises valid. I remember a friend of mine who, in the midst of a very deep trial, could find no comfort in the Scriptures. He asked God for some words of comfort but none came. He finally concluded that though the promises of the Scriptures seemed dead to him, he could trust in the character of God. God fills us with joy as we trust in him.

Consider that absolutely amazing statement of Romans 8:28: in all things God works for the good of those who love him. That statement is true whether you believe it or not. Your faith or lack of it does not determine God's working. He is at work in all the circumstances of your life to bring out the good for you, even if you had never heard of Romans 8:28. His work is not dependent upon your faith. But the comfort and joy that statement is intended to give you is dependent upon your believing it, upon your trusting in him who is at work, even though you cannot see the outcome of that work. God never explained to Job the reason for his trials. He simply brought Job to the place where Job trusted him without an explanation.

Another aid to joy is, *Take the long-range view of life*. The Scriptures repeatedly affirm that the focal point of our joy should be our hope of the eternal inheritance that awaits us in Jesus Christ and the final revelation of his glory. Consider, for example, the following passages:

> In this [hope] you greatly rejoice, though now for a little while you may have had to suffer grief in all kinds of trials. (1 Peter 1:6)
>
> And we rejoice in the hope of the glory of God. (Romans 5:2)
>
> So we fix our eyes not on what is seen, but on what is unseen. For what is seen is temporary, but what is unseen is eternal. (2 Corinthians 4:18)
>
> You . . . joyfully accepted the confiscation of your property, because you knew that you yourselves had better and lasting possessions. (Hebrews 10:34)

To take the long-range view is to rejoice because our names are written in heaven; it is to rejoice in the Lord in whom alone we have the hope of an eternal inheritance that far outweighs whatever troubles we are now experiencing. To take the long-range view is to follow the example of Jesus himself, who "for the joy set before him endured the cross, scorning its shame, and sat down at the right hand of the throne of God" (Hebrews 12:2).

A fourth aid to joy is, *Give thanks in all circumstances* (1 Thessalonians 5:18). This refers, of course, to both pleasant and unpleasant circumstances. We are to be thankful all the time. This does not mean we are to be thankful *for* a difficult circumstance, considered in itself. Rather, we are to give thanks *in the midst of* every circumstance, good or bad. We are to be thankful that God is working in this circumstance for our good. We are to be thankful for past deliverances from trials. We are to be thankful that in this present trial God will not allow a greater burden than we can bear, and that his grace is sufficient to enable us to bear it. And as we give thanks to God we will begin to experience once again the joy that is our heritage in Christ.

The fruits of joy

One of the results of experiencing this joy is that God is pleased (Romans 14:17-18). If Christ came that we might have joy (life to the full), if the Holy Spirit is at work in us to produce joy, then it is a contradiction of God's purpose for us when we are not joyful. Certainly, some people are more joyful by nature than others, but every Christian is to exhibit a balanced display of all the virtues of Christian character, regardless of his temperament. We must look to God and apply all the means he has given us until we can rejoice in the Lord always.

A second result of joy is that we are strengthened physically, emotionally, and spiritually. Nehemiah said to the returned exiles, "Do not grieve, for the joy of the Lord is your strength" (8:10). Sanderson asks, "How much of our physical weakness, apathy and illness is probably due to a heavy spirit?"[4] I have experienced the direct relationship of physical strength to joy in my personal exercise program. When I am rejoicing in the Lord the strength is there, and the jogging and other exercise go much easier. If I am discouraged I seem to have no energy at all.

What is true in the physical or emotional realm is

also true in the spiritual. I recall one morning going into our living room to begin my quiet time. Just prior to that I had been sinning by entertaining resentful thoughts toward a Christian brother. As I started to kneel to pray, the thought came to me, "You cannot enter the presence of God with the thoughts you have been thinking." Thinking of Hebrews 10:19-22, I said, "Lord I acknowledge my sin, and it is true, I cannot come into your presence in my own merit. I come in the only way I can come. I come through the blood of Jesus." As I uttered (and believed) those words I thought, "What a wonderful thing that I, a sinner, having just indulged in the sin of resentment, can through the blood of Jesus come into the very presence of a Holy God." Then I thought, "That's not all! Not only can I come into his presence, but I can call him Father."

That little episode changed my whole day. It changed me from a discouraged, resentful person to a joyous and forgiven person. And the joy of God's gracious forgiveness enabled me to deal with the root of that resentment. Joy does give spiritual strength. The joy of discovering the sufficiency of God's grace enabled Paul to delight in weaknesses, in insults, in difficulties (2 Corinthians 12:9-10).

So the choice is ours. We can be joyless Christians, or we can be joyful Christians. We can go through life bored, glum and complaining, or we can rejoice in the Lord, in our names being written in heaven, in the hope of an eternal inheritance. It is both our privilege and our duty to be joyful. To be joyless is to dishonor God and to deny his love and his control over our lives. It is practical atheism. To be joyful is to experience the power of the Holy Spirit within us, and to say to a watching world, "Our God reigns."

Joy is a fruit of the Spirit. It is a result of his work, but it is also something we must do. We must, by his power, rejoice. This is a part of the practice of godliness.

Notes
1. John W. Sanderson, *The Fruit of The Spirit* (Grand Rapids, Mich.: Zondervan, 1972), page 72.
2. Sanderson, pages 65-66.
3. Sanderson, page 71.
4. Sanderson, page 73.

10
Holiness

THIS IS THE MESSAGE WE HAVE
HEARD FROM HIM AND DECLARE
TO YOU: GOD IS LIGHT; IN HIM
THERE IS NO DARKNESS AT ALL.

1 John 1:5

The outward evidence of godliness is Godlike character. Although it is this character that is usually thought of as godliness, as we have seen in earlier chapters, Godlikeness in character is built upon the foundation of God-centeredness—devotion to God.

If we want to develop godly character, we must learn what the Bible says about the character of God himself. The apostle John gives us two statements about God that together sum up the biblical revelation of God's character: "God is light" (1 John 1:5), and "God is love" (1 John 4:8). The Christian who wants to train himself to be godly must understand the meaning of these statements about the character of God and must appropriate their teachings in his life.

147

What was John telling us about the character of God when he made the statement, "God is light"? Professor Howard Marshall explains, "Two notions became associated with God as light. One was that of revelation and salvation . . . the other is that of holiness; light symbolizes the flawless perfection of God."[1] In 1 John 1:5, it is the idea of God's holiness that is in view. God is absolutely holy; in him there is not the slightest hint of any moral flaw. A well-known soap is advertised as being "99.44 percent pure." While that may be quite an achievement for soap, it would be blasphemous as a statement about God. God is infinitely perfect in his holiness. Not the slightest degree of sin taints his character.

To be Godlike in our character, then, is first of all to be holy. The practice of godliness involves the pursuit of holiness because God has said, "Be holy, because I am holy" (1 Peter 1:16). Paul tells us that we have been called to a holy life; we have been redeemed for that purpose. Any Christian who is not earnestly pursuing holiness in every aspect of his life is flying in the face of God's purpose in saving him.

What is holiness? The best practical definition that I have heard is simply "without sin." That is the statement that was made of the Lord Jesus' life on earth (Hebrews 4:15), and that should be the goal of every person who desires to be godly. Granted, we will never reach that goal in this life; nevertheless it is to be our supreme objective and the object of our most earnest efforts and prayers.

John said he wrote his first letter so that his readers would not sin (1 John 2:1). Most Christians seem content not to sin very much, but John's goal was that we not sin at all. Every sin, no matter how small it may seem to us, is an affront to God's authority, a disregard for his law, a spurning of his love. Because of this, sin cannot be tolerated in any form, to any degree. That "inconsequential" lie, that "just a little bit" of dishonesty, that fleeting lustful look, offends our holy God and wages war against our own souls (1 Peter 2:11).

When Paul was instructing Timothy about his relationship with younger women, he said to treat them "as sisters, with absolute purity" (1 Timothy 5:2). His every thought, look, and act toward them was to be conditioned by a perfect standard of holiness—absolute purity. When Paul was instructing the Ephesian Christians about the importance of holiness he said, "So I tell you this, and insist on it in the Lord, that you must no longer live as the Gentiles do" (4:17). He *insisted* on holiness, and he did so with the Lord's authority. Holiness is not an option but a must for every Christian.

Even for the most godly Christian, there will be failure in the pursuit of holiness. The apostle John says, "If we claim to be without sin, we deceive ourselves" (1 John 1:8). We still have a sinful nature within us, and we still live in a wicked world ruled by a wicked devil. Temptation is on every hand, and our old nature responds to it. But what is the desire of our hearts? What is the object of our most earnest prayers? What is the major bent of our lives? If we want to train ourselves to be godly, it must be holiness in every area of our lives.

But let's get specific. When Paul exhorted the Ephesian Christians to a life of holiness, to stop living as the Gentiles did, he dealt with three general areas of morality: honesty (a refusal to lie, steal, or deceive in any way); peaceableness (freedom from bitterness, anger, or strife of any kind); and purity (not even a hint of sexual immorality in word, look, thought, or act).

We all acknowledge the need for Christians to walk circumspectly in each of these areas. At the same time, we recognize how increasingly difficult it is to do so. Honesty and purity are no longer essential elements of our culture. Lying, cheating, and stealing have become commonplace in business, education, and sports. Sexual immorality is no longer an issue; it is an accepted practice in almost every area of society. And our soaring divorce rate and litigious (a tendency toward lawsuits) society are symptoms of our desperate need for peaceableness.

The Christians of Paul's day lived in the same kind of society; quite possibly it was even worse. Paul said of the non-Christians of Ephesus, "Having lost all sensitivity, they have given themselves over to sensuality so as to indulge in every kind of impurity, with a continual lust for more" (4:19). Things couldn't have gotten much worse in the culture those first-century Christians lived in. Yet in the midst of such gross ungodliness, the Christians were expected to put off the traits of their sinful natures and to put on the traits of righteousness and holiness.

God expects no less of us today. Our responsibility to pursue holiness, even in the midst of a wicked society, is just as great as was the first century Christians'. Yes, it gets more difficult each year; the temptations seem more numerous, the ridicule of the ungodly toward those who seek to live a godly life grows more abusive. But we are still called to be holy as he is holy. We cannot and must not evade God's standard for us.

How do we pursue holiness? Some time ago I heard a seminary professor tell of a friend who would frequently write the letters "YBH" in the margins of books he was reading. When asked what they stood for, he replied, "I agree with the author's challenge to a more consistent Christian life, but my heart says, 'Yes, but how?'" I suspect some of you are asking the same question about holiness—"Yes, but how?"

I have previously mentioned that several years ago God gave me the privilege of writing a book on the subject of holiness. Since its publication, I have had many opportunities to speak on the subject of holiness, often in only a single forty-five-minute message. Because of the necessity of covering such a vast subject in a limited time, I have given much thought to what I think are the most essential elements of holiness. They can be summed up in five words: conviction, commitment, discipline, dependence, and desire.[2]

Convictions: knowledge of the truth

In the passage in Ephesians 4 that we have been considering, Paul says, "be made new in the attitude of your minds." To the Christians at Rome he wrote, "Do not conform any longer to the pattern of this world, but be transformed by the renewing of your mind" (12:2). This process of renewing our minds involves establishing convictions. As we prayerfully expose ourselves to the Scriptures, we begin to understand what God's will is regarding our conduct and character. And then as the Holy Spirit applies his word to specific areas of our lives, and as we are obedient to his promptings, we begin to develop Bible-based convictions. Our values begin to change so that God's standard becomes our delight and our desire.

One has only to prayerfully meditate over Ephesians 4:25—5:7, for example, to realize that God has set down very clear standards regarding honesty, peaceableness, and purity. As we progress in our Christian life, however, we begin to realize more and more the extent of these standards. At first we may be convicted of gross lying; later on we realize that speaking truthfully to our neighbor covers any intent to deceive directly or indirectly; then the Holy Spirit convicts us about "white" lies or social lies that are told to save face or avoid embarrassing someone else.

Each year that we practice godliness the Holy Spirit continues to renew our minds, giving increased understanding of his word and enabling us to develop convictions in greater conformity to his will. Without such Bible-based, Spirit-developed convictions, we easily fall prey to manmade convictions which tend toward one of two extremes. At one extreme is a strict code of legalistic "don'ts" that often miss the more weighty issues of Christian character; at the other is a loose permissiveness that too often conforms to the world's values and customs.

The only safe path is to allow the Holy Spirit to establish convictions through his word. Even on this path, however, we need to be careful not to build convictions upon a misunderstanding of some isolated text of Scripture. Here is where the insight of other

Christians can help us. One of the values of Bible study discussion groups is the opportunity to test our understanding and application of the Scriptures against the thinking of other believers. Godly pastors and teachers who have a gifted insight into the Scriptures can also help us to correctly understand them. Paul himself stated that a part of his calling was to help God's people grow in the knowledge of the truth that leads to godliness.

This is where holiness begins: with the knowledge of the truth that renews our minds and enables us to understand how God wants us to live.

A commitment to obedience

Someone has said, "a belief is what you hold; a conviction is what holds you." A conviction is not truly a conviction unless it includes a commitment to live by what we claim to believe. A commitment is not a vow but a resolution—a determined purpose to live by God's word as he applies it to our lives. First, we need a commitment to holiness as a total way of life. We must decide that holiness is so important to God that it deserves priority attention in our lives. We must commit ourselves to obeying God in all of his commands. We cannot pick and choose according to our own values. A little bit of fudging on one's income tax return is sin just as much as outright theft; an unforgiving spirit toward someone else is sin just as much as murder. I am not suggesting that all sin is equally offensive to God; I am saying that *all* sin is offensive to God. The measure of sin is not just in its effect upon our neighbor, but in its affront to the majesty and holiness of a sovereign God.

Sin is serious business to God, and it becomes serious business to us when we reflect upon the fact that every sin, regardless of how seemingly insignificant it appears to us, is an expression of contempt toward the sovereign authority of God. There is nothing that so motivates me toward a genuine heartfelt confession of sin and a serious resolve to turn from it, as a reflection upon the fact that sin of any degree is an affront to his dignity and a contempt for his law.

The psalmist recognized the seriousness of any and all sin when he said, "You have laid down precepts that are to be fully obeyed" (Psalm 119:4). He recognized that partial obedience—for example, refraining from outright theft of our neighbor's property while allowing our heart to covet it—is actually disobedience. God's precepts are to be *fully* obeyed. And Jesus clearly taught us in the Sermon on the Mount that obedience in our thought life is as necessary as obedience in our actions.

The psalmist's response to his recognition of the seriousness of all sin was a commitment to obedience. He longs that his ways will be steadfast in obeying God's decrees (verse 5). He even takes an oath that he will follow God's righteous laws (verse 106). Clearly, he solidified his convictions about God's will with a determined commitment to obey it.

We need not only a commitment to holiness as a total way of life, but frequently a commitment regarding specific areas of temptation. Job made a personal covenant not to look lustfully at young women (31:1). Daniel resolved not to defile himself with forbidden food, even though from the king's table (1:8). These two Old Testament saints are commended by God himself as among the most righteous who ever lived (Ezekiel 14:14); yet both found it necessary to make a commitment regarding some specific area of temptation. Job found his temptation in his own breast; Daniel found his in his particular circumstances. Both responded with a commitment to obey God. They lived up to their convictions.

The discipline of choices

The third of the five essential elements of holiness is the discipline of daily choices. We have already looked in chapter five at the serious consequences of our daily choices; over time we become what we do. To experience the holiness God calls us to, we must learn to make the right choice in the face of each specific temptation. Paul said the grace of God "teaches us to say 'No' to ungodliness and worldly passions" (Titus 2:11-12). Although he was probably referring to an overall attitude toward sin, and thus to renounce it as a way of life, I find it helpful to take the same attitude toward specific occurrences of temptation. I even go so far as to verbalize (softly or to myself) a firm *no*, at the same time breathing a prayer for the aid of the Holy Spirit to carry through with that choice.

In Romans 8:13, Paul tells us to put to death the misdeeds of the body. We do this by the choices we make—not only to say no to temptations, but also to say yes to the positive steps we must take to pursue holiness. We must exercise ourselves in the disciplines of choosing to feed upon the Scriptures so that our convictions will conform more and more to God's will for us, of choosing to pray constantly for his enabling grace to say no to temptation, of choosing to take all practical steps to avoid known areas of temptation and flee from those that surprise us. These are some of the practical steps we must take to discipline ourselves in holiness. We can easily see that this discipline involves nothing less than an *all-out* effort to turn from every sin and to do the will of God in every area of our lives.

Dependence on the Spirit

Any time we stress the personal responsibility of practical actions, however, we are in danger of thinking that the pursuit of holiness does depend upon our own willpower, our own strength of character. Nothing is further from the truth. We are both *personally responsible and totally dependent* in our practice of godliness. We cannot change our hearts; that is the exclusive work of the Holy Spirit. But we can and must avail ourselves of the means he uses.

In Romans 12:2, we are told to be *transformed* by the renewing of our minds. The word *transformed* means "to be changed within." John Murray says, "The term used here implies that we are to be constantly in the process of being metamorphosed by renewal of that which is the seat of thought and understanding."[3] It is nothing less than a total renovation of our values and desires. This renewal is the exclusive work of the Holy Spirit. Through his ministry we are transformed more and more into the likeness of our Lord. Conceivably, even an unsaved person can change certain actions, but only the Holy Spirit can transform us within; only he can give us new values and desires.

Again the godly writer of Psalm 119 recognizes this dependence upon the Spirit to change his inward thoughts and desires. He prays, "Turn my heart toward your statutes and not toward selfish gain. Turn my eyes away from worthless things; renew my life according to your word" (verses 36-37). This same man who elsewhere in this psalm expresses so strongly his sense of personal responsibility here acknowledges his total dependence upon God for the work of inner transformation. Paul said he had *learned* to be content in every situation. There was no doubt he felt responsible for this changed attitude toward varying circumstances. But he was just as clear that he was totally dependent upon the Holy Spirit working within him to accomplish such a change (Philippians 4:11-13).

This principle of simultaneous personal responsibility and total dependence upon God for fulfillment is one of the most important principles in the practice of godliness. We will not make progress in godliness without consistent application of this principle in our lives.

A God-centered desire
The fifth essential element in the pursuit of holiness is the development of a *God-centered desire* for holiness. We have already considered in chapter five the necessity of a Godward motivation in the development of all the graces of Christian character. The need for such a Godward motivation, however, is especially critical in the pursuit of holiness—the putting off of the sinful traits of the old self. We want victory in our lives, whether it is in a Ping-Pong game or in our struggle with sin. We want to feel good about ourselves, and we know we will not as long as we are

allowing some sin to gain mastery over us.

To paraphrase a writer from a previous century, so often when we sin we are more vexed at the lowering of our self-esteem than we are grieved at God's dishonor. We are irritated at our lack of self-control in subjecting ourselves to some unworthy habit. We are unable to stand the disappointment of seeing ourselves fail.

God does not honor these self-centered desires. This is one reason we do not experience more of his enabling power in our day-to-day struggles with so-called besetting sins. God does not give us his power so that we might feel good about ourselves; he gives us his power so that we can obey him for his sake, for his glory. It is not wrong to feel good about ourselves, but this should be a byproduct of obedience which is motivated by a desire to please God.

We have learned in earlier chapters that godliness is first of all God-centeredness. This concept is extremely important in the area of holiness. Our desire for holiness, our motivation to pursue it, must be a God-centered desire and motivation. Developing this God-centered motivation requires practice or training; it does not come naturally or easily. We are by nature self-centered. If we are diligent to examine ourselves, we will often find that our motivation is self-centered. We must confess and renounce this, just as we must any disobedient action, and then seek a God-centered motivation.

___

Notes
1. Howard Marshall, "The Epistles of John," *The New International Commentary on the New Testament*

(Grand Rapids, Mich.: Eerdmans, 1978), page 109.
2. These five essentials, as well as other aspects of
   holiness, are more fully developed in *The Pursuit of
   Holiness* (NavPress, 1978). This book may be
   obtained from most local Christian bookstores or by
   contacting NavPress at P.O. Box 6000, Colorado
   Springs, Colo. 80934.
3. John Murray, "The Epistle to the Romans," *The
   New International Commentary on the New Testament*, Vol. II (Grand Rapids, Mich.: Eerdmans,
   1965), page 114.

11
Self-Control

LIKE A CITY WHOSE WALLS ARE
BROKEN DOWN IS A MAN WHO
LACKS SELF-CONTROL.

Proverbs 25:28

In ancient times the walls of a city were its main defense; without them the city was easy prey to its enemies. To godly Nehemiah, a Jewish captive in the faraway city of Susa, the news that the wall of Jerusalem was broken down signified the ultimate destruction of his beloved city. When he heard the news he sat down and wept.

Self-control is the believer's wall of defense against the sinful desires that wage war against his soul. Charles Bridges has observed that the person without self-control is easy prey to the invader: "He yields himself to the first assault of his ungoverned passions, offering no resistance. . . . Having no discipline over himself, temptation becomes the occasion of sin, and hurries him on to fearful lengths

161

that he had not contemplated. . . . Anger tends to murder. Unwatchfulness over lust plunges into adultery."[1]

Self-control is control *of* one's self. It is probably best defined as *the governing of one's desires*. D.G. Kehl describes it as "the ability to avoid excesses, to stay within reasonable bounds."[2] Bethune calls it "the healthful regulation of our desires and appetites, preventing their excess."[3] Both of these descriptions imply what we all know to be true; we have a tendency to overindulge our various appetites and consequently need to restrain them.

But self-control involves a much wider range of watchfulness than merely control of our bodily appetites and desires. We also must exercise self-control of thoughts, emotions, and speech. There is a form of self-control that says *yes* to what we should do as well as that which says *no* to what we shouldn't do. For example, I seldom *want* to study the Bible when I first begin a study. There are too many other things that are mentally much easier to do, such as reading the newspaper, a magazine, or a good Christian book. A necessary expression of self-control, then, is to set myself down at the dining room table with Bible and notebook in hand and say to myself, "Get with it!" This may not sound very spiritual, but neither does Paul's exclamation, "I beat my body and make it my slave" (1 Corinthians 9:27).

Self-control is necessary because we are at war with our own sinful desires. James describes those desires as dragging us away and enticing us into sin (1:14). Peter says they war against our souls (1 Peter 2:11). Paul speaks of them as deceitful (Ephesians

4:22). What makes these sinful desires so dangerous is that they dwell within our own heart. External temptations would not be nearly so dangerous were it not for the fact that they find this ally of desire right within our own breast.

Self-control is an essential character trait of the godly person that enables him to obey the words of the Lord Jesus, "If anyone would come after me, he must deny himself and take up his cross daily and follow me" (Luke 9:23). It is impossible to be a follower of Jesus without giving diligent attention in our lives to the grace of self-control.

The translators of the *New International Version* of the Bible have used the expression *self-control* to translate two different words from the original language. The first word, which is used by Paul in his list called the fruit of the Spirit, refers primarily to moderation or temperance in the gratification of our desires and appetites. A friend of mine who is a former teacher of Greek says it has the literal meaning of "inner strength," and refers to that strength of character that enables one to control his passions and desires.

The second word rendered *self-control* by the NIV translators is a word that denotes soundness of mind or sound judgment. It is rendered *sober* or *sensible* by other translations. This word conveys the idea of allowing sound judgment to control our desires and appetites, our thoughts, emotions, and actions.

We can readily see that these two ideas complement one another in the biblical meaning of self-control. Sound judgment enables us to determine what we should do and how we should respond; inner strength provides the will to do it. Both sound judgment and inner strength are thus necessary for Spirit-directed self-control.

Sound judgment is critical to the exercise of self-control. It enables the godly person not only to distinguish good from evil, but also to sort out the good and the best. Sound judgment enables us to determine the boundaries of moderation in our appetites, desires, and habits. Sound judgment helps us regulate our thoughts and keep our emotions under control.

But sound judgment alone is not enough to enable us to practice self-control. Inner strength is also essential. All too often we know very well *what* to do, but we do not do it. We allow feelings or desires to overrule our judgment. Ultimately, *Self-control is the exercise of inner strength under the direction of sound judgment that enables us to do, think, and say the things that are pleasing to God.*

Since the grace of self-control affects so many aspects of our lives, it is helpful to focus study of it in three major areas: body, thoughts, and emotions.

Honor God with your body

"And the Lord God made all kinds of trees grow out of the ground—trees that were pleasing to the eye and good for food" (Genesis 2:9). God created man to enjoy sensuous pleasures; that is, things that are pleasant to our senses and bodily appetites. The trees of his creation where not only good for food, but also pleasant to the eyes. There is no doubt that God intends that we enjoy the physical things of this life which he has so graciously provided. As Paul says in

1 Timothy 6:17, "God . . . richly provides us with everything for our enjoyment."

But man in his sin has corrupted all of the natural blessings which God has given. Because our desires have been corrupted, those things which God intended for our use and enjoyment have a tendency to become our masters. Paul had to warn the Corinthian believers against this tendency when he said, " 'Everything is permissible for me'—but I will not be mastered by anything" (1 Corinthians 6:12). The moderation resulting from self-control keeps permissible things from becoming masters of our bodies.

In the rather short letter in which Paul instructs Titus in his pastoral duties among the Cretan Christians, Paul frequently refers to the grace of self-control. It is a requirement for elders, it is important for older men, younger men, older women and younger women; it is in fact to be a characteristic of all believers. Why did Paul so stress this trait of self-control? Because the Cretans were "always liars, evil brutes, lazy gluttons" (1:12). They were demonstrably in need of the grace of self-control. Someone characterized as a lazy glutton certainly needs to learn self-control of the body.

Self-control of the body should be aimed primarily at three areas of physical temptation: gluttony (in both food and drink), laziness, and sexual immorality or impurity. Although drunkenness is a widespread sin in the non-Christian culture of today, I do not detect that it is a major problem among Christians. But gluttony surely is. Most of us have a tendency to overindulge in the food which God has so graciously provided for us. We allow the sensual part of our God-given appetite to range out of control and lead us into sin. We need to remember that even our eating and drinking is to be done to the glory of God (1 Corinthians 10:31).

What about laziness? Most of us would no doubt assent to the widespread need for self-control with respect to food and drink among Christians today. But laziness? I suspect we don't particularly think of ourselves collectively as a lazy people like those Cretan Christians. We work hard at our jobs, keep our houses painted and our lawns trimmed. Can we have a problem with laziness?

To answer that question, let's look at an incident in the life of Jesus. Mark records that "Very early in the morning, while it was still dark, Jesus got up, left the house and went off to a solitary place, where he prayed" (1:35). That Jesus got up to pray while it was still dark is challenging enough. But note what had happened the night before. Mark tells us that on the previous evening after sunset the people brought to Jesus all the sick and demon-possessed to be healed; the whole town, in fact, gathered at the door (verses 32-34). Jesus was probably quite weary at the end of that evening.

Now you and I, under those circumstances, would have tended to sleep in the following morning, feeling that after such a full evening of ministry we deserved a rest and a little pampering. But not Jesus. He knew the importance of getting that time of fellowship with his Father, and he disciplined his physical body in order to do it.

I suspect that the number of Christians who have a consistent, productive time of fellowship with God each day is a very small minority. For some, such a time is non-existent; for others, it is sporadic at best. This is because we tend to be lazy in body and undisciplined in the use of our time.

There are other Christians who have learned the self-control of getting up in the morning to have fellowship with God, but who haven't learned the self-control of caring for their bodies. Some are abusing their bodies through a constant lack of needed rest and recreation; others are allowing their bodies to become soft and flabby through no exercise at all. Both groups need to learn godly self-control of their bodies.

Sexual self-control belongs to both the body and the mind. There was a time, a generation or so ago, when we would hardly have felt it necessary to exhort Christians to exercise self-control in the area of sexual immorality. Control of impure thoughts, yes; but even the more moral segment of non-Christian society condemned the actual physical acts of immorality. This situation no longer exists. Authorities in our social and psychological areas today are telling us that premarital or extramarital sexual activity is okay as long as it is not emotionally harmful.

Many Christians, unfortunately, are falling prey to such thinking. Immorality among both single and married people is becoming a major concern in the Christian community. The need for sexual self-control among Christians has probably never been greater since the rise of the first-century Gentile church out of gross paganism.

God's standard for sexual self-control is *absolute abstinence* outside of the marriage relationship. If, as

Kehl suggests, self-control is the ability to stay within reasonable bounds, then we must realize that God's boundary for sexual activity is limited strictly to marriage. As Hebrews 13:4 says, "Marriage should be honored by all, and the marriage bed kept pure, for God will judge the adulterer and all the sexually immoral." Paul's words to the Thessalonian believers also leave no room for compromise on this point: "It is God's will that you should be holy; that you should avoid sexual immorality; that each of you should learn to control his own body in a way that is holy and honorable, not in passionate lust like the heathen, who do not know God" (1 Thessalonians 4:3-5).

The Christian must exercise self-control not only in the area of sexual activity, but in the area of impure thoughts, lustful looks, and suggestive speech as well. Jesus said, "I tell you that anyone who looks at a woman lustfully has already committed adultery with her in his heart" (Matthew 5:28). A lustful look quickly becomes an impure thought. If *acts* of immorality are becoming a problem among Christians, the *thoughts* of immorality are a much greater problem. Sexual lust lies latent in the heart of every Christian. Even righteous Job found it necessary to deal decisively with this temptation; he made a covenant with his eyes not to look lustfully at a girl (31:1). If Job found it necessary to make this kind of commitment in the day in which he lived, how much more do we need it in today's society—where sexual lust is exploited even to advertise spark plugs!

The subject of control of our bodies, then, especially in the area of sexual purity, leads naturally to a second area of self-control: our thoughts.

Take captive every thought

Paul said, "We take captive every thought to make it obedient to Christ" (2 Corinthians 10:5). Although the immediate context indicates that he was referring to the thoughts of his opponents at Corinth, it still remains a worthy objective for the control of our own thoughts. Self-control of our thoughts means entertaining in our minds only those thoughts that are acceptable to God.

The best guideline for evaluating the control of our thoughts is that given by Paul in Philippians 4:8: "Finally, brothers, whatever is true, whatever is noble, whatever is right, whatever is pure, whatever is lovely, whatever is admirable—if anything is excellent or praiseworthy—think about such things." Self-control of our thoughts, then, is more than just refusing to admit sinful thoughts—such as lust, greed, envy, or selfish ambition—into our minds. Controlling our thoughts also includes focusing our minds on that which is good and pleasing to God.

Solomon warned us, "Above all else, guard your heart, for it is the wellspring of life" (Proverbs 4:23). The meaning of the Hebrew word for "heart" generally refers to our entire conscious person—understanding, emotions, conscience, and will; the warning is particularly applicable, however, to our thought life. It is in our thought life that our emotions and actions begin, and that sinful desires plant their roots and entice us into sin.

Our minds are mental greenhouses where unlawful thoughts, once planted, are nurtured and watered before being transplanted into the real world of unlawful actions. People seldom fall suddenly into gluttony or immorality. These actions are savored in the mind long before they are enjoyed in reality. The thought life, then, is our first line of defense in the battle of self-control.

The gates to our thought lives are primarily our eyes and our ears. What we see or read or hear largely determines what we think. Memory, of course, also plays a big part in what we think, but our memories only store and feed back what originally comes into our minds through our eyes and ears. Guarding our hearts begins with guarding our eyes and ears. We must not allow that which panders to sexual lust, greed (called materialism in our present society), envy, and selfish ambition to enter our minds. We should avoid television programs, magazine or newspaper articles, advertisements, and conversations that arouse such thoughts. We should not only avoid them, but, to use Paul's words to Timothy, "flee from all this." It is well worth noting that in both of his letters to Timothy, Paul felt it prudent to warn Timothy to *flee* temptation. Although Timothy was a godly leader, he was not exempt from the necessity of exercising self-control.

Solomon said to *guard*; Paul said to *flee*. Both verbs convey a much stronger reaction to temptation than most Christians practice. Instead of guarding the gates of our minds, we actually open them to the flood of ungodly material coming to us through television, newspapers and magazines, and the world's conversations that often surround us. Instead of fleeing from temptations, we too often indulge them in our thoughts.

We allow in our minds what we would not allow

in our actions, because other people cannot see our thoughts. But God sees them. David said, "You perceive my thoughts from afar," and "Before a word is on my tongue you know it completely, O Lord" (Psalm 139:2,4). The Christian who fears God, controls his thoughts—not because of what other people think, but because of what God thinks. He prays, "May the words of my mouth and the meditation of my heart be pleasing in *your* sight, O Lord, my Rock and my Redeemer" (Psalm 19:14).

The television and printed media are not the only culprits in leading our thoughts astray. Paul's checklist for controlled thoughts in Philippians 4:8 includes such requirements as "true" and "noble" as well as "pure." A Christian may not be particularly bothered with impure thoughts, but may be tempted to entertain those that are not true or noble. Listening to such things as gossip, slander, or criticism about others needs to be rejected just as strongly as the tendency to pass them over our tongues.

It is impossible to listen in a condoning manner to gossip or criticism about someone else and then think only thoughts that are true and noble about that person. And if we guard our thoughts we will more easily guard our tongues, for Jesus said, "For out of the overflow of the heart the mouth speaks" (Matthew 12:34).

Curbing our emotions
The emotions that need to be controlled include anger and rage (the so-called "hot temper"), resentment, self-pity, and bitterness. The feelings may be explosive, as in the case of an uncontrolled temper, or

they may be only simmering, as in the case of self-pity. But in either case these emotions are displeasing to God and need to be included in our efforts to exercise self-control.

An uncontrolled temper is a contradiction in the life of a person who is seeking to practice godliness. Outbursts of temper are harmful not only because they release our own ungoverned, sinful passions, but more importantly because they wound those who are the recipients of such outbursts. In this respect temper is a unique challenge in the area of self-control. Ungoverned thoughts and other emotions are sins within our own minds; they harm only ourselves, unless of course they lead to sinful words or actions. But an uncontrolled temper damages the self-respect of others, creates bitterness, and destroys relationships.

We are of course talking here about an *uncontrolled* temper. Many believers by temperament have a tendency to lash out at those who incur their displeasure in some way. But the godly person has learned to control this tendency. Solomon said, "Better a patient man than a warrior, a man who controls his temper than one who takes a city" (Proverbs 16:32). To have a temper that requires control is not a mark of ungodliness; to fail to control it is. To succeed, by God's grace, in controlling an unruly temper is to demonstrate godly self-control.

Someone has said of Proverbs 16:32, "Note what price the Holy Spirit puts on a curbed temper; it is more to be sought than a decisive victory in war." Charles Bridges has commented, "The taking of a city is child's play, compared with this wrestling. . . .

That is only the battle of a day. This, the weary, unceasing conflict of a life.''[4] The person who painfully struggles, often with failure, to control his temper should take to heart God's evaluation of this struggle and be willing to pay the price necessary to succeed in it.

Although not as harmful to others, other uncontrolled emotions such as resentment, bitterness, and self-pity may be more destructive to ourselves and to our relationship to God. Uncontrolled temper is soon dissipated on others. Resentment, bitterness, and self-pity build up inside our hearts and eat away at our spiritual lives like a slowly spreading cancer.

All of these sinful inner emotions have in common a focus on self. They put our disappointments, our wounded pride, or our shattered dreams on the thrones of our hearts, where they become idols to us. We nurture resentment and bitterness, and we wallow in self-pity. Intellectually we know that in all things God works for our good, that nothing can separate us from his love. But in defiance of those God-given promises, we *choose* to think about that which is dishonoring to God and destructive of our own spiritual health.

Just as the apostle Paul beat his body (figuratively speaking, of course), so we must subdue our sinful emotions. We must deal decisively with them at their first appearance in our thoughts. Keeping a tight rein on our emotions is just as necessary to godliness as keeping the appetites and desires of our bodies under control.

Breaking the chains of self-indulgence

The emphasis in the struggle for self-control should be on the word *growing*. We will never fully attain self-control in all areas in this life. Furthermore, we must realize that the battle of self-control is different for each of us. One person may have no problem at all with bodily self-control, but he may struggle with thoughts of spiritual pride. Another may never be bothered with impure thoughts but may indulge his emotions in resentment or in self-pity. As we are tempted to judge others for their lack of self-control in areas where we have no problems, let us remember our own areas of struggle and be charitable in our opinions.

Sound judgment is the beginning of self-control, and the Bible is absolutely essential to its exercise. Sound judgment must be based on a thorough knowledge of God's standard, as revealed in the Scriptures, for our bodies, thoughts, and emotions. Years ago when I first began to grow as a Christian I read the quotation, "God's word will keep you from sin, or sin will keep you from God's word." This is not simply a cliché, nor is the Bible some magical wand to wave at temptation. It is sound judgment, growing out of reflection on the word of God, that warns us when the enemy of sinful desire is assaulting the citadel of our hearts.

Sound judgment also enables us to form an accurate estimate of our particular needs in the area of self-control. Paul's admonition, "think of yourself with sober judgment" (Romans 12:3), is good advice, not only for assessing our spiritual gifts, but also for assessing our spiritual needs. Proverbs 27:12 says, "The prudent see danger and take refuge." Spiritual prudence requires that we know ourselves—our particular weaknesses and vulnerabilities. Only as we study both the Scriptures and ourselves will we be able to exercise sound judgment.

Next, we must face the issue of whether we are truly willing to give up enjoying the fleeting pleasures of sin in return for knowing that our lives are pleasing to God. Kehl points out, "The beginning of self-mastery is to be mastered by Christ, to yield to his lordship. 'Wouldst thou have thy flesh obey thy spirit?' Augustine asked. 'Then let thy spirit obey thy God. Thou must be governed, that thou may'st govern.'"[5] Are you willing to acknowledge Jesus Christ as Lord of your appetites and desires, of your thoughts and emotions? If self-control begins with sound judgment, it must be carried forward by surrender to the authority of Christ in every area of our lives.

Then we must realize that the battle for self-control is fought primarily within our own minds; it is a battle with our own passions, thoughts, and desires. In those areas where we have failed to curb our appetites and emotions, we seem to have invisible antennae sensitively attuned to the corresponding temptations. The proverbial "chip on his shoulder" describes the person whose antenna is constantly searching for the minor incident that he can magnify into an occasion for losing his temper. The person who habitually yields to some bodily appetite or lust is constantly alert for opportunities to indulge that carnal desire. We must learn to say no to those passions when they first enter our minds.

Above all, we must pray for the inner strength of will necessary to curb our passions and desires. It is God who works in us to will and to act. Our own particular areas of vulnerability must be made the subject of earnest, beseeching prayer for God's grace to work in our wills. At the same time we must realize that the will is strengthened by obedience. The more we say no to sinful desires, the more we will *be able* to say no. But to experience this, we must persevere through many failures. A large part of learning self-control is breaking bad habits and replacing them with good ones. And this process always involves a certain amount of failure.

Finally, as Kehl points out, "True spiritual self-discipline holds believers in bounds but never in bonds; its effect is to enlarge, expand and liberate."[6] James describes the word of God as "the perfect law that gives freedom" (1:25). As we grow in the grace of self-control, we will experience the liberation of those who, under the guidance and grace of the Holy Spirit, are freed from the shackles of self-indulgence and are brought into the freedom of true spiritual discipline.

Notes

1. Charles Bridges, *An Exposition of Proverbs* (1846; rpt. Evansville, Indiana: Sovereign Grace Book Club, 1959), page 483.
2. D. G. Kehl, *Control Yourself!* (Grand Rapids, Mich.: Zondervan Publishing House, 1982), page 25. This is an excellent book for those who want to pursue the subject of self-control further.
3. Bethune, *The Fruit of the Spirit*, page 179.
4. Charles Bridges, page 250.
5. Kehl, page 79.
6. Kehl, page 26.

12
Faithfulness

MANY A MAN CLAIMS TO HAVE
UNFAILING LOVE, BUT A FAITHFUL
MAN WHO CAN FIND?

Proverbs 20:6

Opening my concordance to the word *faithfulness*, I quickly ran my finger down the column and counted more than sixty references in the Bible to the faithfulness of God. It is not surprising that some forty of these instances occur in the book of Psalms, which recounts, more than any other book in the Bible, the struggles of the godly and their total dependence upon God's faithfulness.

Consider for a moment the absolute necessity of the faithfulness of God. We are dependent upon his faithfulness for our final salvation (1 Corinthians 1:8-9), for deliverance from temptation (1 Corinthians 10:13), for ultimate sanctification (1 Thessalonians 5:23), for the forgiveness of our sins (1 John 1:9), for deliverance through times of suffering

(1 Peter 4:19), and for the fulfillment of our ultimate hope of eternal life (Hebrews 10:23). We can easily see that every aspect of the Christian life rests upon the faithfulness of God, and we have the assurance, "The Lord is faithful to all his promises" (Psalm 145:13).

No wonder, then, that the psalmist says, in reflecting upon the faithfulness of God,

> with my mouth I will make your faithfulness known through all generations. I will declare . . . that you established your faithfulness in heaven itself. (Psalm 89:1-2)

Even the prophet Jeremiah, in the midst of his lamentations over the judgment of God upon Judah, could still proclaim of God, "Great is your faithfulness" (Lamentations 3:23).

Actually, even a study of the sixty references to the faithfulness of God couldn't do justice to the subject: The entire Bible is a treatise on that theme. God's faithfulness appears in precept or illustration on almost every page. It is impossible to describe the acts of God without in some way touching upon his faithfulness to his own.

In our effort to become like God in our character, we must ensure that the grace of faithfulness is very high in our value system. This is not a natural virtue, as indicated by Solomon's lament, "Many a man claims to have unfailing love, but a faithful man who can find?" (Proverbs 20:6). Many people will profess faithfulness, but very few will demonstrate it. The virtue of faithfulness is often costly, and few people are willing to pay the price. But for the godly person, faithfulness is an absolutely essential quality of his character, regardless of what it might cost.

What is faithfulness? How do we practice it, and when do we exhibit it in our lives? The biblical word denotes that which is firm and can be counted upon. The dictionary defines *faithful* as "firm in adherence to promises or in observance of duty."[1] Some common synonyms are "dependable," "reliable," "trustworthy," and "loyal." The word also has the connotation of absolute honesty or integrity.

The faithful person is one who is dependable, trustworthy, and loyal, who can be depended upon in all of his relationships, and who is absolutely honest and ethical in all of his affairs. It was said of Daniel that his rivals "tried to find grounds for charges against Daniel in his conduct of government affairs, but they were unable to do so. They could find no corruption in him, because he was trustworthy [faithful] and neither corrupt nor negligent" (Daniel 6:4).

The words *corrupt* and *negligent* help us define, by contrast, what it means to be faithful in our daily affairs. The word *corrupt* is the opposite of "honest" or "ethical," and the word *negligent* is an antonym of such words as "careful," "thoughtful," and "considerate."

Absolute honesty

Daniel was not corrupt; he was honest, ethical, and principled. Absolute honesty in speech and in personal affairs has to be the hallmark of a faithful person. The Scriptures tell us, "The Lord detests lying lips, but he delights in men who are truthful," and

"The Lord abhors dishonest scales, but accurate weights are his delight" (Proverbs 12:22 and 11:1). The Lord detests lying and abhors dishonest business transactions. Not only are we commanded not to lie; we are also commanded not to deceive in any manner (Leviticus 19:11).

Lying has been defined as "any deceit: in word, act, attitude—or silence; in deliberate exaggerations, in distortions of the truth, or in creating false impressions."[2] We lie or deceive when we pretend to be something we are not; when as students we cheat on an examination, or as taxpayers we fail to report all of our income. My friend Jerry White writes of struggling over how much to tell a prospective buyer about a used car.[3] The issue of honesty pervades every area of our lives.

On Christmas Eve our doorbell rang, and when I answered it, I found a little four-year-old neighbor girl holding out a plate of cookies. "My mommy sent you some cookies," she said with a big smile. I thanked her and put the cookies down someplace—and promptly forgot about them, for we were just leaving for a Christmas Eve church service. A few days later as I was walking out to my car, the little girl came down the sidewalk on her tricycle. "Mr. Bridges, how'd you like the cookies?" she asked in great anticipation. "Oh, they were fine," I said, though I had not even tasted them.

As I drove away I began to think about what I had said. I had lied; there was no question about it. Why had I done it? Because it was expedient; it saved me embarrassment and the little girl disappointment (though mostly I was concerned about myself, not

her). Sure, it was only a social lie, of little or no conse-
quence. But it was a lie, and God says without qualification that he detests lying.

As I thought of that incident I began to realize it
wasn't an isolated instance. The Holy Spirit reminded me of other occasions of seemingly innocent
"social lying," of instances of exaggeration, or
manipulating the facts of a story just a bit. I had to
face the fact that I was not quite as honest as I had considered myself to be. God taught me a valuable,
though humbling, lesson through that plate of
cookies.

As I have told the story of the cookies to some au-
diences, I have gotten a troubled reaction from a few
people. Some people, sincere Christians, think I may
be nitpicking, going a bit too far in this matter of absolute honesty. But consider Daniel. The record states
that his enemies could find no corruption in him. It
seems clear that these government officials, from
their bitter jealousy and utter hostility toward Daniel,
would have seized upon any inconsistency, regardless
of how small or insignificant, to bring Daniel into
disrepute before King Darius. But they could find
none. Daniel, like Elijah, was a man with a nature just
like ours (James 5:17), but he had evidently mastered
this matter of absolute integrity. We should have the
same goal.

Think of the Lord Jesus. One day he asked his
enemies, "Can any of you prove me guilty of sin?"
(John 8:46). If Jesus had ever distorted the truth even
a little bit, he could not have asked that question with
such total confidence. We are called to be like Jesus—
to be as absolutely honest as he was. How would Jesus

have handled the little neighbor girl's question about the cookies? I don't know what he would have said. But one thing I know; he would not have lied. And neither should you or I.

Why do I go into such detail about absolute honesty in the social minutiae of life? Because this is where honesty begins. If we are careful to be honest in the little things, we will certainly be careful to be honest in the more important things of life. If we are honest about the cookies in our lives, we will certainly be honest in our business transactions, our college examinations, and even our sports competitions. As Jesus said, "He who is faithful in a very little thing is faithful also in much; and he who is unrighteous in a very little thing is unrighteous also in much" (Luke 16:10 NASB).

Our age desperately needs to reemphasize honesty in both its business transactions and its social intercourse. I recall reading an article in one of our leading business journals that quoted a number of executives as saying it was impossible to succeed in business today without compromising the truth. Probably the same attitude prevails in politics, sports, and every other aspect of our society. But we Christians are called to be salt in a putrefying society, and we cannot be such if we are not models of absolute honesty.

Utter dependability

Daniel was neither corrupt nor negligent: He was reliable and dependable. People could count on him. He undoubtedly was on time for his appointments, kept his commitments, honored his word, and considered how his actions might affect others.

Few things are more vexing than relying on someone who is not dependable. Solomon observed, "As vinegar to the teeth and smoke to the eyes, so is a sluggard to those who send him" (Proverbs 10:26). Though the term *sluggard* refers to a habitually lazy person, it is his unfaithfulness that makes him exasperating. We may be indifferent about a lazy person's habits if we do not have to rely on him. But if we are dependent upon his actions in any way, we see his slothful habits as unfaithfulness.

If our society needs to reemphasize the virtue of honesty, it certainly needs to place great importance on dependability. Dependability has taken a decided back seat to personal desire or convenience. "I'll keep that commitment if it's convenient," seems to be the attitude of our age. John Sanderson has perceptively observed,

> If we probe a bit deeper, we see that "unfaithfulness" is very close to "disobedience," for the man who disobeys God has cast himself loose from the only solid support a man can have, and his direction in life will be controlled by the shifting winds of circumstances and of his whimsical desire. . . . The man who is not controlled by God has no settled reason to keep his word or discharge his obligations.[4]

For the person who is practicing godliness, then, dependability is a duty owed not only to his fellow man, but more importantly to God. Reliability is not just a social obligation; it is a spiritual obligation. God is even more concerned about our faithfulness than the person who is relying on us in some particular situation.

In Psalm 15, David asks the question, "Lord, who may dwell in your sanctuary? Who may live on your holy hill?" There follows a list of ethical standards that a person must keep to enjoy God's fellowship. And in the middle of that list there is this standard: He "who keeps his oath even when it hurts." God wants us to be dependable even when it costs us. This is what distinguishes godly faithfulness from the ordinary dependability of secular society.

Consider the teenager who agrees to baby-sit for a neighbor on a given evening. Then a young man calls and invites her to the football game on that same night. What is she to do? Does she just simply cancel her baby-sitting arrangement and leave the neighbor to find someone else? The godly teenager will keep her commitment even when it hurts. Or, she might seek to find a substitute agreeable to the neighbor. In either case she feels a responsibility before God to honor her commitment and to fulfill her responsibility.

Lest I appear to be singling out teenagers as especially vulnerable to the temptation to treat commitments lightly, consider the businessman who enters into an agreement only to discover that it is quite to his disadvantage. What is he to do? The non-Christian is most apt to contact his lawyer to see if there is some legal loophole through which he can get out of the contract. Unfortunately, many Christians will seek the same relief. Not so the godly businessman. He may indeed see if there is some resolution to his dilemma that is acceptable to the other party. But he will not renege on his word just because it is legally possible to do so. He will keep his word even when it hurts.

Between these two extremes of the merely inconvenient baby-sitting engagement and the financially disastrous business agreement, there are numerous instances in which all of us make commitments that from time to time may prove costly to keep. At times such as these we especially need, by God's grace, to manifest the fruit of the Spirit that is faithfulness.

Unswerving loyalty

The faithful person is not only honest and dependable, but also loyal. As an issue, loyalty arises most often in connection with our friends. The word has come to have a connotation of sticking with someone through thick and thin. There is perhaps no greater description of loyalty than Solomon's words, "A friend loves at all times, and a brother is born for adversity" (Proverbs 17:17).

There is no such person as a "fair-weather friend." If a person's loyalty doesn't insure his faithfulness to another in times of stress, then he really isn't a friend. He is simply using the other person to satisfy some of his own social needs.

King Saul's son, Jonathan, provides probably the best illustration of loyalty in the Bible. His loyal friendship with David almost cost him his life at the hands of his own father. Amazingly, Jonathan realized that his loyalty to David would, in the end, cost him the throne of Israel. Whether it be in honesty or dependability or loyalty, faithfulness is frequently a costly virtue. Only the Holy Spirit can enable us to pay that price.

There is a kind of loyalty that we must avoid, however: a so-called "blind loyalty." This kind refuses to admit the mistakes or faults of a friend, and it is actually a disservice. Proverbs tells us, "The kisses of an enemy may be profuse, but faithful are the wounds of a friend" (Proverbs 27:6). Only the truly faithful friend cares enough about you or me to undertake the often thankless task of pointing out where we are wrong. None of us enjoys being confronted with our faults or sins or mistakes, so we often make it difficult for our friends to do so. As a result, most of us are more concerned about speaking agreeableness to each other than about speaking the truth. This is *not* loyalty. Loyalty speaks the truth in faithfulness, but it also speaks it in love. Loyalty says, "I care enough about you that I will not allow you to continue unchecked in your wrong action or sinful attitude that will ultimately be harmful to you."

Meeting God's requirement

As with the other graces of Christian character, the first step in growing in faithfulness is to acknowledge the biblical standard. Faithfulness entails absolute honesty, utter dependability, and unswerving loyalty. It is to be like Daniel: neither corrupt nor negligent. Develop convictions consistent with this standard based on the word of God. Plan to memorize one or more verses on the topic of faithfulness, either from the references cited in this chapter, or from others that may have come to your mind.

Second, evaluate your life with the aid of the Holy Spirit and perhaps a spouse or close friend. Do you seek to be scrupulously honest? Can others depend on you even when it is costly? Will you stick by your friend when he is in difficulty, and will you confront him in love when he is wrong? Don't be satisfied with generalities. Try to think of specific instances that either affirm your faithfulness or show you where you need to grow.

Where you see a specific need for faithfulness, make that both a matter of prayer for the aid of the Holy Spirit and the object of some concrete actions on your part. Remember that your working and his working are coextensive. You cannot become a faithful person merely by trying. There is a divine dimension. But it is also true that you will not become a faithful person without trying. Jesus said to the church in Smyrna, "Be faithful, even to the point of death" (Revelation 2:10). This is something we must do, even though it is at the same time the fruit of the Spirit.

Consider the reward for faithfulness. In the parable of the talents, the master replied, "Well done, good and faithful servant! You have been faithful with a few things; I will put you in charge of many things. Come and share your master's happiness!" (Matthew 25:21). It may be argued that the faithfulness here is in relation to God, rather than to one another, as we have been discussing in this chapter. That is indeed true. But faithfulness to God *includes* faithfulness to one another. That is the ultimate point of each of the Scripture passages we have considered. It is God who requires that we be faithful in all of our earthly relationships. So only if we seek to grow in the grace of faithfulness toward one another, will we have any hope of hearing him say "Well done, good and faithful servant."

Notes

1. *Webster's New Collegiate Dictionary* (Springfield, Mass.: G. & C. Merriam, 1974).
2. As quoted in *Character of the Christian: Book four of the Studies in Christian Living*, 1st ed. (Colorado Springs: NavPress, 1964), page 26.
3. Jerry White, *Honesty Morality & Conscience* (Colorado Springs: NavPress, 1978), page 53. I highly recommend this book for further study on the topic of honesty.
4. Sanderson, *The Fruit of the Spirit*, page 117.

13
Peace

IF IT IS POSSIBLE, AS FAR AS IT
DEPENDS ON YOU, LIVE AT PEACE
WITH EVERYONE.

Romans 12:18

Untold millions of dollars are spent annually in search of peace. Every year thousands of people seeking personal or family peace flock to professional counselors. Diplomats fly around the world pursuing peace between nations. Our court systems are jammed with cases arising from a breakdown of peace between individuals or corporations.

Christians are not exempt from this turmoil of a sinful world. We, too, experience the anxiety of disquieting circumstances and the anguish of broken relationships.

But peace should be a hallmark of the godly person, first because it is a Godlike trait: God is called the God of peace several times in the New Testament. He took the initiative to establish peace with rebellious

189

men, and he is the author of both personal peace as
well as peace among men. Peace should be part of our
character also because God has promised us his peace,
because he has commanded us to let peace rule in our
lives and relationships, and because peace is a fruit of
the Spirit and therefore an evidence of his working in
our lives.

A close look at Scripture reveals that peace is actually threefold:

- peace with God
- peace within ourselves
- peace with other people.

These are not three parallel but unrelated types of
peace; rather, they are three different expressions of
one peace—the peace that God gives, which is called
the fruit of the Spirit. These different facets complement and reinforce one another, producing an overall
character trait. Each aspect has unique characteristics
that contribute in varying ways to the life of a man or
woman of peace.

Peace with God

The basis of our peace with God is our justification by
faith in Jesus Christ. Scripture says, ''Therefore, since
we have been justified through faith, we have peace
with God through our Lord Jesus Christ'' (Romans
5:1). This is the point at which all peace begins. We
cannot have peace within or peace with other people
until we first have peace with God.

Prior to our salvation, because we were born in
sin, our relationship to God was characterized by
alienation and enmity (Colossians 1:21). We were
objects of his wrath, in a state of rebellion against

him. Even though the religious stupor in which we lived and the particular circumstances which surrounded us may have given us a false sense of peace, in reality we were "like the tossing sea, which cannot rest, whose waves cast up mire and mud," because, as God has said, "there is no peace for the wicked" (Isaiah 57:20-21).

Upon entering a personal relationship with God through faith in Jesus Christ, however, all this changes. Instead of being opposed to us, God is now for us. Instead of leaving us to the mercy of circumstances, he promises to work in all of them for our good (Romans 8:28). Proverbs 16 tells us that he even promises to make our enemies live at peace with us.

Peace with God, then, is the foundation of peace within ourselves and peace with other people. This foundation does not guarantee, of course, that these other aspects of peace occur automatically. We must pursue what makes for peace, both within and without, in dependence upon the Holy Spirit, realizing that the fruit of peace is his fruit, not ours.

Personal peace

One of the petty offenses for which we arrest people is disturbing the peace. Even though a Christian has experienced peace *with* God, there are certain "disturbers of the peace" that keep him from experiencing the peace *of* God. Like the noisy or quarrelsome offenses against society, these disturbers are often petty in nature. The more calamitous events in our lives usually force us to turn to the Lord with all our hearts, and, in so doing, we experience his grace and peace. But the more ordinary adversities of life rob us of peace because we have a tendency to try to deal with these events ourselves. We worry, fret, and scheme over distressing circumstances, and we envy or resent other people who appear to get a better deal in life, or who mistreat us in some way.

As Jesus finished talking to his disciples on the evening of his betrayal, he concluded with these words: "I have told you these things, so that in me you may have peace. In this world you will have trouble. But take heart! I have overcome the world" (John 16:33). In this assurance of peace Jesus made two promises.

His first promise was that we will have trouble in the world. The same circumstances that rob us of our joy also rob us of our peace. The common denominator of all these circumstances is uncertainty. A loved one is ill, and the diagnosis is uncertain. Or our car breaks down while on a trip; will we have enough money to pay for repairs and perhaps extra meals and lodging? How will we get to our destination in time? Our luggage fails to arrive with us on an airline flight. Will we ever see it again? What will we do until it is returned to us? These and countless other circumstances continue to prove that Jesus was indeed correct when he promised us that we will have trouble in the world.

But the second promise that Jesus made was just as correct. He has overcome the world. Ephesians 1:22 tells us that "God placed all things under his feet and appointed him to be the head over everything for the church"; that is, Jesus has been appointed head over everything *on behalf of* the church. He has power over all the universe, and he exercises it on our behalf and for our good. In Matthew 10:29-31, Jesus tells us that not even a sparrow can fall to the ground apart from the will of our Father. And even the very hairs of our head are all numbered. No detail is too small or minute that it escapes the Father's eye and attention. And now Jesus in his ascended glory exercises that same watchful care on our behalf.

So why do we worry? Because we do not believe. We are not really convinced that the same Jesus who can keep a sparrow in the air knows where our lost luggage is, or how we are going to pay that auto repair bill, or how we can get to our destination on time. Or if we believe that he *can* deliver us through our difficulties, we doubt if he *will*. We let Satan sow seeds of doubt in our minds about his love and care for us.

Two passages of Scripture will prove most helpful to us in coming to him to find peace. The first is Philippians 4:6-7: "Do not be anxious about anything, but in everything, by prayer and petition, with thanksgiving, present your requests to God. And the peace of God, which transcends all understanding, will guard your hearts and your minds in Christ Jesus." The great antidote to anxiety is to come to God in prayer. We are to pray about *everything*. Nothing is too big for him to handle, and nothing is too small to escape his attention.

Paul also declares that we are to come to God with thanksgiving. We should thank him for his past faithfulness in delivering us from troubles (remembrance of past mercies is a great stimulus to present faith). We should thank him for the fact that he is in control of every single circumstance of our lives, and that nothing can touch us that he does not allow. We should thank him that in his infinite wisdom he is able to work in this circumstance for our good, and that because of his love, he would not have allowed it if it were not for our good. Finally, we can thank him that he will not allow us to be tempted (either a seduction to evil, or a trial of our faith; both ideas are included in the word) beyond what we can bear (1 Corinthians 10:13).

The result promised to us when we come to God in prayer with thanksgiving is not deliverance, but the peace of God. One of the reasons we don't find this peace is because all too often we will not settle for anything other than deliverance *from* the trouble. But God, through Paul, promises us peace, a peace that is unexplainable. It transcends all understanding. And, says Paul, it will guard our hearts and minds against the anxiety to which you and I are so prone.

Now if you are like me, you are probably thinking, "That all sounds very nice, and I agree with you intellectually right now. But when I am in the midst of a trying situation, I really don't experience that peace. What's wrong?"

I suggest two steps to take when in this kind of dilemma. First, examine your motives—you may want deliverance instead of peace. Are you looking for the wrong answer? Second, look to the Holy Spirit to bring you that peace. Remember, peace is the fruit of the Spirit. It is his work to produce peace within you. Your responsibility is to come in prayer, asking for the peace, and looking to him for it.

I doubt that any Christian is more vulnerable to worry and fretfulness than I am. I sympathize with others who are also prone to anxiety. I am well aware that it is only by the power of the Holy Spirit that we can experience his peace. But God tells us in his word that his peace is available, and we must not be content until we experience it. We must persevere in prayer until he answers.

In addition to Philippians 4:6-7, a second passage of Scripture that can help us deal with anxiety is 1 Peter 5:7-9: "Cast all your anxiety on him because he cares for you." In the next verse Peter tells us to be alert to the devil, who prowls around looking for someone to devour. One of the many ways in which the devil tries to devour us is related to the meaning of his name. The Greek word for devil means "accuser," or "slanderer." As the prince of slanderers, he accuses man before God, but he also slanders God to man. One of the thoughts that often enters our minds when we are undergoing some trial is, "If God really loved me he would not have allowed this to happen to me." Or, "If God loved me, he would provide a way out of this trying situation."

Such thoughts come from the devil; failure to recognize this origin causes two problems. First, we assume those thoughts originate within our own hearts, so we add a sense of guilt for thinking harsh thoughts about God to our already anxious mind. Now we have both anxiety and guilt to contend with, compounding our problem. Second, we fight the wrong battle. Instead of resisting the devil, we try to deal with our own wicked hearts. Although there are plenty of times when we do have to deal with our own wicked hearts, this is not one of them: this is a time to resist the devil. We have a very clear command, coupled with a promise: ''Resist the devil, and he will flee from you'' (James 4:7).

This is the Bible's solution to a lack of peace within ourselves: Take our anxieties to God in thankful prayer, and resist the devil when he slanders God to us. Only when we have experienced peace *with* God, through bringing our anxieties to him, are we able to deal with the third aspect of peace: peace with other people. Inner conflict and turmoil often result in conflict with others, so we must achieve inner peace to effectively pursue peace with others.

Peace with men

When Paul listed peace as one of nine traits of the fruit of the Spirit, he was probably thinking primarily of peace with other people. He had already warned the Galatians against ''biting and devouring each other'' (Galatians 5:15). And in his list of the acts of the sinful nature, immediately preceding his list of the fruit of the Spirit, those actions that are totally opposite to peace are predominant: hatred, discord, jealousy, fits of rage, selfish ambition, dissensions, factions, and envy. As he began to list traits of godly character that the Galatians needed to keep foremost in mind, peace with one another must have been near the top of his list.

The importance of this aspect of peace is amply evident from major references to it in the New Testament. Here are just a few:

Blessed are the peacemakers. (Matthew 5:9)

As far as it depends on you, live at peace with everyone. (Romans 12:18)

Make every effort to do what leads to peace.
(Romans 14:19)

Let the peace of Christ rule in your hearts, since as
members of one body you were called to peace.
(Colossians 3:15)

Make every effort to live in peace with all men.
(Hebrews 12:14)

Whoever would love life and see good days . . .
must seek peace and pursue it. (1 Peter 3:10-11)

Three times in these references we are exhorted to
"make every effort" toward, or "pursue," peace.
The Greek word used here also means "persecute,"
conveying the idea of intense effort or vigilance in
tracking down something in order to harass and torment. In a positive sense, it means singleminded pursuit: to leave no stone unturned in our efforts, to lay
ourselves out and to humble ourselves, if need be, in
order to achieve the goal of peace with others.

The pursuit of peace does not include an easy-
going, peace-at-any-price kind of attitude; it does not
include capitulating to wrong or injustice just for the
sake of maintaining appearances. That kind of behavior often leads instead to strife within ourselves.
The conflicts that are disturbing our peace with others
must be courageously but graciously faced and dealt
with. Pursuing peace does not mean running away
from the causes of discord.

Let's consider some practical, biblical steps we
can take to pursue peace in conflicts with other believers:

First, *We must remember that we are fellow*

members of the same body. Paul says, "The body is a unit, though it is made up of many parts; and though all its parts are many, they form one body. So it is with Christ" (1 Corinthians 12:12). Farther on in the same chapter he says the goal is "so that there should be no division in the body, but that its parts should have equal concern for each other" (verse 25). It is incredible that different parts of the same body could be at war among themselves! I am convinced that there would be much less disharmony and conflict among believers if we constantly kept in mind that we are members of the same body.

Paul puts it even more strongly in Romans 12:5: "each member belongs to all the others." Not only are we members of the same body, but we *belong* to one another. That person with whom you have difficulty maintaining peace belongs to you, and you belong to him. What a contradiction to the unity of the body when there is discord among its members.

Not only must we remember that we are fellow-members of one body, *We must also keep in mind that it is Christ's body of which we are members.* It is *his* glory—and the honor of *his* church—that is at stake in our relationships with one another. Few things are as dishonoring to the cause of Christ as Christians quarreling among themselves. Yet we expel people from our fellowship for adultery, while we tolerate discord between ourselves and other believers. We have failed to understand and obey the biblical imperative to "make every effort to do what leads to peace."

Third, *We must recognize that the cause of discord often lies wholly or partly with us.* We must seek a genuine spirit of humility about our own responsibility rather than entirely blaming the other person. On occasion, I have been an observer to discord between believers in which both parties wholly blamed the other for the conflict. Neither was willing to accept any responsibility for a misunderstanding. As we pursue peace we must be prepared to face up to and acknowledge to the other party any wrong attitude, action, or words on our part.

Finally, *We must take the initiative to restore peace.* Jesus taught that it makes no difference whether you have wronged your brother or he has wronged you. Either way, *you* are always responsible to initiate efforts toward peace (see Matthew 5:23-24 and 18:15). If we are serious about intently pursuing peace, we won't be concerned about which of us is the offending party. We will have one goal: to restore peace in a godly manner. Unresolved conflict between believers is sin and must be treated as such; otherwise, it will spread throughout the body like cancer until it requires radical spiritual surgery. Far better to deal with it when it is easily contained.

There may be times, however, when you have pursued peace to no avail. The Bible recognizes that possibility (Romans 12:18), but be sure you have done all you can to restore peace.

The "going to your brother" of Matthew 5 and Matthew 18 relates to conflict among believers; pursuing peace with unbelievers requires a somewhat different approach. Obviously, we are not members of one body. We do not share the work of the Holy Spirit in enabling us to restore peace. How, then, should we handle conflict with unbelievers?

First, *If we have offended an unbeliever, it is our responsibility to take steps to restore peace.* Sometimes this is more humbling than going to a believer to acknowledge a wrong; the unbeliever is not as apt to respond in a gracious and forgiving manner. But humbling or not, we must do this if we are to maintain a Christian testimony.

What should we do, however, when the unbeliever wrongs us? When there is no common bond, no fellowship to be restored, no mutual presence of the Holy Spirit to aid in restoration, then we tend to think in terms of revenge—if not in action, at least in our thoughts.

I believe Romans 12:17-21 provides the answer. As we look at this passage we see that first, *We are to do everything we possibly can to maintain peace*, as far as it depends on us.

Second, *We are in no way to seek revenge.* We are not to repay evil for evil; we are to leave the matter of justice in the hands of God. So often when we have been wronged, or think we have been wronged, we imagine getting even with the other person. We don't *intend* to take revenge, but we actually do it in our minds. Such an attitude is clearly contrary to Scripture. Verse 19 says that it is God's prerogative to mete out justice; his judgment alone is always according to the truth. He alone knows all the facts and all the motives behind them.

As we are willing to leave justice with God, we have his assurance that he will repay. God is a God of infinite justice; no wrong inflicted on us ever goes unnoticed by him. Although we may never be aware of the repayment, we do have God's promise of it.

Of course, our goal with regard to an offending unbeliever should not be a desire for revenge, either God's revenge or ours. The purpose of God's assurance of justice here is not to satisfy our own sense of justice, but to remove it as a consideration from our minds. God in effect is saying, "Don't concern yourself with justice. Leave that to me. You concern yourself with something else: winning over the offending unbeliever." We can win him over, or at least make an effort to do so, by repaying evil with good. However we may understand the expression "heap burning coals on his head" (verse 20), it seems clear that our intent should be to win him over.

Because peace is a fruit of the Spirit, we are dependent upon the Spirit's work in our lives to produce the desire and the means to pursue peace. But we are also responsible to use the means he has given us and to take all practical steps to attain both peace within and peace with others.

Commit to memory such passages of Scripture as Philippians 4:6-7, 1 Peter 5:7, Romans 12:18, or any others you find especially helpful. Begin to meditate upon them and ask the Holy Spirit to bring them to your mind on the next occasion in which you especially need to follow their teaching. Remember that practicing godliness involves spiritual exercise—meditating upon and applying God's word under the directon of our teacher, the Holy Spirit.

14
Patience

CLOTHE YOURSELVES WITH . . .
PATIENCE. BEAR WITH EACH
OTHER AND FORGIVE WHATEVER
GRIEVANCES YOU MAY HAVE
AGAINST ONE ANOTHER.

Colossians 3:12-13

Christian character is like a single garment woven from threads of varying colors and shades. From a distance the garment appears to be a single color, but closer examination reveals that it takes a combination of different colored threads to produce the overall effect. The casual observer is not too concerned with those various threads; he notices and appreciates the garment's overall effect. But the creator of that cloth has to consider each thread individually, ensuring that the right shades and colors correctly follow the pattern of the design.

Some of the traits of godly character appear to blend together much as different shades of thread in a garment or colors in a rainbow. Patience, for example, closely resembles joy and peace in its effect upon our lives. The word *patience*, as we use it in everyday speech, actually stands for several different words in the New Testament, and is used to describe a godly reaction to a variety of situations. These different words and usages blend together to produce an overall quality.

The truly patient Christian must display godly patience in all of the various circumstances requiring it. Just as the designer and weaver of a beautiful cloth must consider each thread individually, so the Christian who desires to grow in patience must give attention to each facet of this quality as it applies to his life.

Suffering mistreatment

One aspect of patience involves enduring abuse. The biblical response to suffering at the hands of others is called *long-suffering* in the *King James Version*, and that rendering perhaps best describes its meaning. This aspect of patience is the ability to suffer a long time under the mistreatment of others without growing resentful or bitter. The occasions for exercising this quality are numerous; they vary from malicious wrongs all the way to seemingly innocent practical jokes. They include ridicule, scorn, insults, and undeserved rebukes, as well as outright persecution. The Christian who is the victim of office politics or organizational power plays must react with long-suffering. The believing husband or wife who is rejected or mistreated by an unbelieving spouse needs this kind of patience.

The apostle Paul especially stressed the need for long-suffering in the life of a godly person. He mentions it in his first letter to the Corinthians, in his list of qualities that characterize love. He includes it as one of the nine traits which he calls the fruit of the Spirit in Galatians. When he describes to the Ephesians a life worthy of God's calling, he includes the the trait of long-suffering. He also includes it when he gives the Colossians a list of godly qualities with which Christians should clothe themselves. He stresses it to the Thessalonians, and commends his own life to the Corinthians and to Timothy partly because patience is one of his character traits.

How can we grow in this aspect of patience, that suffers long under the ill-treatment of others? First, we must consider the *justice* of God. In his instructions to slaves who needed to be patient under the unjust treatment of harsh masters, Peter tells them to follow the example of Christ: "When they hurled their insults at him, he did not retaliate; when he suffered, he made no threats. Instead, he entrusted himself to him who judges justly" (1 Peter 2:23). Note that the opposite of retaliation is to entrust ourselves to God, who judges justly. God's justice is absolute, and, as Paul reminds us in Romans 12:19, he promises us, "I will repay."

One of the thoughts that most disturbs a suffering Christian who has not learned patience is this issue of justice. He is concerned that his tormentor will escape justice, that he will not receive the punishment he deserves. The patient Christian who suffers leaves this issue in the hands of God. He is confident that God will render justice, though he knows that this may not occur until the time of our Lord's return (2 Thessalonians 1:6-7). Instead of hoping and waiting for an opportunity for revenge, he prays for

God's forgiveness of his tormentors, just as Jesus and the martyr Stephen prayed for their executioners.

To develop patience in the face of mistreatment by others, we must also develop a conviction about the *faithfulness* of God to work on our behalf. Peter tells us that ''those who suffer according to God's will should commit themselves to their faithful Creator and continue to do good'' (1 Peter 4:19). We should entrust ourselves to God's justice and commit ourselves to his faithfulness. God will deal not only in justice (and we pray, in mercy) with our tormentor, but also in faithfulness with us.

Joseph exemplified such a commitment to the faithfulness of God. After he had been abused by his brothers, he was able to say to them, ''You intended to harm me, but God intended it for good to accomplish what is now being done, the saving of many lives'' (Genesis 50:20). God can and does take the deliberately harmful acts of others and turn them into acts for good, both for us and for others. The person who is patient under mistreatment by others is the person who has developed such a confidence in the wisdom, power, and faithfulness of God that he willingly entrusts his circumstances into his hands.

Responding to provocation

The aspect of patience that is called long-suffering is also used to describe the response of the godly person to provocation by others. I use the word *provocation* to denote those actions of others that tend to arouse our anger or wrath—that cause us to lose our temper. Unlike mistreatment by others, which is often out of our control, provocation finds us in a position of power to do something about it. It may come in the form of defiance of our authority—a parent, teacher, or supervisor on a job—or it may be a deliberate goading or nagging of us. Whatever form the action takes, it is often deliberate, and we are in a position to retaliate or punish swiftly and harshly.

When we exercise patience under provocation we are emulating God himself. In Exodus 34:6-7, God describes himself as "slow to anger . . . forgiving wickedness, rebellion and sin." Daily, God bears with great patience the provocation of sinful, rebellious men who despise his authority and ignore or show contempt for his law. It is to these very people that Paul addresses the question, "Do you show contempt for the riches of his kindness, tolerance and patience?" (Romans 2:4). They despise not only his authority, but his patience. And yet God continues to show the *riches* of his patience to those who least deserve it.

The key to patience under provocation is to seek to develop God's own trait of being "slow to anger." James tells us to be "slow to become angry" (James 1:19). Paul says that one characteristic of love is that it is not "easily angered" (1 Corinthians 13:5).

The best way to develop this slowness to anger is to reflect frequently on the patience of God toward us. The parable of the unmerciful servant (Matthew 18:21-35) is designed to help us recognize our own need of patience toward others by recognizing the patience of God toward us. In this parable, the unmerciful servant was deeply indebted to his master—according to the *New International Version*, by several million dollars. The king of the parable obviously represents God, while the deeply indebted servant represents each of us in our relationship to God as sinners. As the parable develops, the first servant is completely forgiven of his huge debt. But just after he leaves the presence of his master, he finds a fellow servant who owes him only a few dollars, and impatiently demands payment—even having the man thrown into prison.

We are like the unmerciful servant when we lose our patience under provocation. We ignore God's extreme patience with us. We discipline our children out of anger, while God disciplines us out of love. We are eager to punish the person who provokes us, while God is eager to forgive. We are eager to exercise our authority, while God is eager to exercise his love.

This kind of patience does not ignore the provocations of others; it simply seeks to respond to them in a godly manner. In enables us to control our tempers when we are provoked and to seek to deal with the person and his provocation in a way that tends to heal relationships rather than aggravate problems. It seeks the ultimate good of the other individual, rather than the immediate satisfaction of our own aroused emotions.

The person whose temperament is conducive to losing his temper must especially work at patience under provocation. Rather than excusing himself by saying, "that's just the way I am," he must acknowledge his quick temper as a sinful habit before God. He should meditate extensively upon such verses as Exodus 34:6, 1 Corinthians 13:5, and James 1:19. He must also pray earnestly that God the Holy Spirit will change him inwardly. He should apologize to the person who is the object of his outburst *each time* he loses his temper. (This helps him develop humility and a sense of his own sinfulness before God.) Finally, he must not become discouraged when he fails. He needs to realize that his problem is as much a sinful habit as it is a result of temperament. Habits are not easily broken, and there will be failure. But, in the words of Proverbs 24:16, "No matter how often an honest man falls, he always gets up again . . ." (*Good News Bible*).

Tolerating shortcomings

It is likely that most of us have occasion to show patience toward the faults and failures of others more often than we do toward mistreatment or provocation from others. People are always behaving in ways that, though not directed against us, affect us and irritate or disappoint us. It may be the driver ahead of us who is driving too slowly, or the friend who is late for an appointment, or the neighbor who is inconsiderate. More often than not it is the unconscious action of some family member whose irritating habit is magnified because of close daily association. The kind of patience it takes to overlook these circumstances is probably demanded of us most often within our own families or Christian fellowships.

Impatience with the shortcomings of others often has its roots in pride. John Sanderson observes, "Hardly a day passes but one hears sneering remarks about the stupidity, the awkwardness, the ineptitude of others."[1] Such remarks stem from a feeling that we are smarter or more capable than those with whom we are impatient. Even if that is actually true, Paul tells us in 1 Corinthians 4:7 that whatever abilities we possess have been given to us by God, so we have no reason to feel that we are any better than anyone else.

The patient reaction to the faults and failures of others is probably best described by the word *forbearance*, as it is used in Ephesians 4:2 and Colossians 3:13 (KJV). Literally, the word can mean "to put up with" and can be used in a negative sense of grudging endurance of another's faults. That is obviously *not* the sense in which Paul uses the word. Rather, he uses forbearance in the sense of gracious tolerance of another's faults. Since forbearance is not a common word in the daily vocabulary of most people, the word *tolerance* is probably best used to describe this aspect of patience.

Forbearance or tolerance in the Scriptures is associated with love, the unity of the believers, and the forgiveness of Christ. In Ephesians 4:2-3 Paul says, "Be completely humble and gentle; be patient, *bearing with one another in love*. Make every effort to keep the unity of the Spirit through the bond of peace." Peter tells us that "love covers over a multitude of sins"; love for the other person causes us to overlook or tolerate his shortcomings.

I recall an instance when a friend of mine forgot an appointment we had together. Rather than being peeved, I simply shrugged it off. Later I tried to determine why I had had such a tolerant reaction to his failure. I concluded it was because I deeply loved and appreciated this person, and the principle that Peter stated—"love covers over a multitude of sins"—was at work.

Paul says we are to bear with one another in order to preserve the "unity of the Spirit"—the unity applied by the Spirit to the body of Christ. We are to *make every effort* to maintain this unity. We are to consider the unity of the body far more important than the petty irritants or disappointments of others. Again, as in maintaining peace, Romans 12:5 is very helpful: "each member belongs to all the others." When I am tempted to become irritated with my brother in Christ, remembering that he belongs to me, and that I belong to him, helps quell that budding sense of exasperation.

In Colossians 3:13 Paul equates forbearance with forgiveness: "Bear with each other and forgive whatever grievances you may have against one another." The thought of grievances or complaints used in this verse seems to connote the idea of fault-finding with petty actions rather than concern over more serious problems. Instead of letting those actions irritate us, we are to use them as an opportunity to forgive as the Lord forgave us.

The principle of forgiving as the Lord forgave us is taught in the parable of the unmerciful servant. The main point of that parable lies in the tremendous contrast between the two debts: several million dollars versus a few dollars. Jesus also makes a point of the timing of the two encounters: the unmerciful servant, fresh from the forgiving presence of his master, turns around and harshly demands immediate payment from his debtor.

How well this parable depicts us when we are impatient with others! Every day God patiently bears with us, and every day we are tempted to become impatient with our friends, neighbors, and loved ones. And our faults and failures before God are so much more serious than the petty actions of others that tend to irritate us! God calls us to graciously bear with the weaknesses of others, tolerating them and forgiving them even as he has forgiven us.

Such scriptural forbearance does not forbid correcting another's faults or confronting someone about an irritating habit. Rather, Jesus teaches us that such correction should be done with the right attitude. We are not to seek to remove the speck of sawdust—that irritating habit or fault—from our brother's eye until we have first removed the plank from our own eye. The plank in our eye can be any wrong attitude toward our brother that is a reaction to his fault or weakness. It may be irritation, pride, or a critical or disdainful attitude. Whatever our wrong attitude may be, we must first deal with it, making sure our desire to correct or confront is not from a spirit of impatience, but from a spirit of love and concern for the welfare of the other person.

Waiting on God

Another area in which most of us need to learn patience is in the outworking of God's timetable in our lives. Perhaps we have been praying for many years for the salvation of a loved one, for the resolution of some problem we face, or for the fulfillment of some long-awaited desire. Abraham's long wait for the birth of his son, Isaac, is the classic biblical illustration of the need for patience to await God's timing. Like Abraham, many of us have attempted to speed up God's timetable or to substitute another solution as Sarah and Abraham did with Ishmael, only to end up with sorrow instead of fulfillment.

Saul is another example of one who would not wait for the fulfillment of God's timetable, and for this he lost his kingdom. Both Abraham and Saul grew impatient because of unbelief in the faithfulness of God and an unwillingness to wait on him. God, in his sovereign grace, gave Abraham another chance and so he became the father of those who believe.

In contrast to Saul, David waited for the Lord to fulfill his plan for him. He consistently refused to take matters into his own hands, instead saying,

> I waited patiently for the Lord;
>> he turned to me and heard my cry.
> He lifted me out of the slimy pit,
>> out of the mud and mire;
> he set my feet on a rock
>> and gave me a firm place to stand. (Psalm 40:1-2)

James addresses the problem of waiting by referring first to the patience of the farmer who waits for his crop, then to the patience of the prophets who all died without seeing the fulfillment of most of their prophecies, and finally to the patience of Job, who in the end did experience the Lord's deliverance. The ultimate event for which we all wait, of course, is the Lord's coming. With the apostle John, we cry in our hearts, "Come, Lord Jesus" (Revelation 22:20).

The cure for impatience with the fulfillment of God's timetable is to believe his promises, obey his will, and leave the results to him. So often when God's timetable stretches into years we become discouraged and give up. I think of a desire of mine that I thought God would soon fulfill. When several years went by, I virtually gave up, but in the seventh year, God answered that prayer. I think of another answer to prayer that has occurred just recently. I had been praying for that request for so many years that when the answer finally came, I felt it was too good to be true. I think of still another God-given desire that I prayed over for some thirteen years before God answered. But when he did, the answer came in abundant measure.

Yet in spite of these long-awaited answers to prayers, I still struggle with impatience over God's timetable. I still want to give up or try to work something out on my own. I need to take to heart this admonition of the writer of Hebrews: "We do not want you to become lazy, but to imitate those who through faith and patience inherit what has been promised" (6:12). If you struggle, as I do, with the patience of waiting, that might be a good verse for you to memorize and meditate over in the months ahead.

Persevering through adversity

Whereas long-suffering should be our patient reaction to *people* who mistreat or provoke us, endurance and perseverance should be our patient reaction to *circumstances* that try us. *Endurance* is the ability to stand up under adversity; *perseverance* is the ability to progress in spite of it. These two English words are translations of the same Greek word and simply represent two different views of the same quality: a godly response to adversity.

The source of adversity may be the ill-treatment

of other people, as when Joseph's brothers sold him into slavery, or when Saul persecuted David, or when the Jews rejected and crucified the Lord Jesus. At other times our trials are a result of Satan's attacks, as in Job's case. Still another source of adversity is the direct disciplinary hand of God in our lives.

Whatever the source of our adverse circumstances, the key to endurance and patience is to believe that God is ultimately in control, working out events for our good. Romans 15:4 says, "For everything that was written in the past was written to teach us, so that through endurance and the encouragement of the Scriptures we might have hope." The stories of Abraham, Jacob, Joseph, David, and Job were written so that we might have the privilege of seeing God at work, controlling their circumstances for their good and his glory. These examples should encourage us to believe that God controls our circumstances as well, even though we do not always recognize this control. For many years it has helped me to realize that God never explained to Job why his trials had occurred. You and I are taken behind the scenes and shown the battle between God and Satan. But Job never knew. He simply came to the place where he accepted whatever God allowed. Most often, we do not see the purpose of trials. But through the encouragement of the Scriptures we should hope, and through hope we should persevere.

Endurance and perseverance are frequently associated with hope in the Scriptures. In each of four instances in which Paul speaks of perseverance or endurance in Romans, it is in the context of hope. He commends the Thessalonian believers for their endurance inspired by hope. And the entire treatment of endurance and perseverance by the writer of Hebrews closely links endurance and perseverance with hope (see especially chapters 10—12). Hebrews 11, the great chapter on faith, is a part of this lengthy challenge to endurance and perseverance; it begins by defining faith as "being sure of what we hope for and certain of what we do not see."

The object of this hope, of course, is our ultimate glorification with Christ in eternity. The life we live on this earth is simply a pursual of this hope. The author of Hebrews likens it to a distance race which must be run with perseverance. Our Christian experience is not a sprint that is soon over; it is a distance race that lasts a lifetime. It requires perseverance, because the reward—the object of our hope—is in the distant future.

Endurance and perseverance are also frequently associated with suffering in the Bible. We may not like this connection, because we may shrink from the suffering, but we must come to terms with it. Endurance can be produced only under stress, whether physical or spiritual. In Romans, Paul says suffering produces perseverance. James says trials that test our faith develop perseverance. Endurance and perseverance are qualities we would all like to possess, but we are loath to go through the process that produces them. That is why God is so faithful to allow or to bring trials into our lives, even though we shrink from them.

So we see that God uses the encouragement of the Scriptures, the hope of our ultimate salvation in glory, and the trials that he either sends or allows to produce endurance and perseverance. He also works directly in our hearts. In Romans 15:5, Paul tells us that God gives endurance and encouragement. We know from verse 4 that God uses the Scriptures, but he must also work directly, making those Scriptures meaningful and personally applicable to us. When Paul prayed that the Colossians would have great endurance and patience, he was counting upon God to work directly in their hearts. We cannot explain this direct ministry in the heart of the believer, but that does not make it any less valid. The Bible constantly affirms this direct ministry of the Spirit of God (for example, see Romans 8:26-27, 2 Corinthians 1:3-4, and Ephesians 3:16-19).

The fruit of patience in all its aspects—longsuffering, forbearance, endurance, and perseverance—is a fruit that is most intimately associated with our devotion to God. All character traits of godliness grow out of and have their foundation in our devotion to God, but the fruit of patience must grow out of that relationship in a particular way. Only as we fear God will we submit to the trials he sends or allows. And only as we deeply apprehend his love for us in Christ will we find the courage to bear up under them. Trials always change our relationship with God. Either they drive us to him, or they drive us away from him. The extent of our fear of him and our awareness of his love for us determine in which direction we will move.

Notes
1. Sanderson, *The Fruit of the Spirit*, page 90.

15
Gentleness

THE FRUIT OF THE SPIRIT IS . . .
GENTLENESS.
CLOTHE YOURSELVES WITH . . .
GENTLENESS.

Galatians 5:22-23 and Colossians 3:12

We pray for patience, we pray for love, we pray for purity and self-control. But who of us ever prays for the grace of gentleness? Writing in the year 1839, George Bethune said, "Perhaps no grace is less prayed for, or less cultivated than gentleness. Indeed it is considered rather as belonging to natural disposition or external manners, than as a Christian virtue; and seldom do we reflect that not to be gentle is sin."[1]

The Christian attitude toward gentleness does not seem to have changed in the more than 140 years since Bethune penned those words. I once asked a co-worker in our own ministry if he was aware of anyone who was praying for or seeking to cultivate gentleness. He thought for a moment, and said no. This is not to say that the grace of gentleness is entirely absent from the Christian community; but perhaps we don't value it as highly as God values it.

Gentleness is somewhat difficult to define, because it is often confused with meekness, which is another Christian virtue that we should pursue. Billy Graham defines gentleness as "mildness in dealing with others . . . it displays a sensitive regard for others and is careful never to be unfeeling for the rights of others."[2] Gentleness is an active trait, describing the manner in which we should treat others. Meekness is a passive trait, describing the proper Christian response when others mistreat us.

Gentleness is illustrated by the way we would handle a carton of exquisite crystal glasses; it is the recognition that the human personality is valuable but fragile, and must be handled with care.

Both gentleness and meekness are born of power, not weakness. There is a pseudo-gentleness that is effeminate, and there is a pseudo-meekness that is cowardly. But a Christian is to be gentle and meek because those are Godlike virtues. Isaiah 40 is a chapter that describes both the power and the tenderness of God:

> See, the Sovereign Lord comes with power. . . .
>   (verse 10)
> Surely the nations are like a drop in a bucket;
>   they are regarded as dust on the scales;
>   he weighs the islands as though they were fine
>   dust. (verse 15)
> "To whom will you compare me?
>   Or who is my equal?" says the Holy One.
> Lift your eyes and look to the heavens:

Who created all these?
He who brings out the starry host one by one,
    and calls them each by name.
Because of his great power and mighty strength,
    not one of them is missing. (verses 25-26)

Tucked in the middle of this description of God's power are these words:

He tends his flock like a shepherd:
    He gathers the lambs in his arms
and carries them close to his heart;
    he gently leads those that have young. (verse 11)

The same passage that stresses the infiniteness of God's power also beautifully portrays his gentleness. What better illustrates gentleness than a shepherd carrying his lambs close to his heart? Yet the Holy Spirit uses this word picture, framed with illustrations of sovereign power, to describe God. We should never be afraid, therefore, that the gentleness of the Spirit means weakness of character. It takes strength, God's strength, to be truly gentle.

An interesting and enlightening variation between translations of a phrase in Psalm 18:35 helps define true gentleness. The *New American Standard Bible* and the *King James Version* translate David's declaration, "Thy *gentleness* makes me great." The *New International Version* renders it, "you *stoop down* to make me great." Gentleness is stooping down to help someone. God continually stoops down to help us, and he wants us to do the same—to be sensitive to the rights and feelings of others.

The gentleness of Christ

Paul appealed to the Corinthian Christians "By the meekness and gentleness of Christ" (2 Corinthians 10:1). How does the New Testament describe the gentleness of Christ?

A very familiar passage in Matthew provides a picture of Christ's gentleness:

> Come to me, all you who are weary and burdened, and I will give you rest. Take my yoke upon you and learn from me, for I am gentle and humble in heart, and you will find rest for your souls. For my yoke is easy and my burden is light. (Matthew 11:28-29)

William Hendriksen says that the Syriac New Testament translates the word *gentle* as "restful"; accordingly Jesus' expression is, "Come to me . . . and I will *rest* you . . . for I am *restful* . . . and you shall find *rest* for yourselves."[3] Christ's whole demeanor was such that people were often restful in his presence. This effect is another outworking of the grace of gentleness. People are at rest, or at ease, around the Christian who is truly gentle.

Matthew 12:20 gives us another picture of the gentleness with which Christ treats us: "A bruised reed he will not break, and a smoldering wick he will not snuff out, till he leads justice to victory." The bruised reed and the smoldering wick refer to people who are hurting, spiritually weak, or of little faith. Jesus deals gently with such people. He does not condemn them for their weakness; he does not come down with a "heavy hand"; rather, he deals with them gently until their true need is exposed and they

are open to him for help. How beautifully his encounter with the Samaritan woman illustrates his
gentleness. Firmly, yet gently, Jesus continued to
probe her need until she recognized it herself and
turned to him to meet it.

In the very act of his appeal to the Corinthians by
"the meekness and gentleness of Christ," Paul illustrated that gentleness for us. We could paraphrase
his remarks as, "Acting as Christ would act in this
situation I appeal to you. I do not demand; I do not
insist, but I *appeal* to you." Paul could have berated
the Corinthians for allowing into their fellowship
those who sought to undermine his apostolic authority, but he didn't; instead, he chose to exercise the
Spirit-produced fruit of gentleness.

When Paul wrote to the Philippians, "Your attitude should be the same as that of Christ Jesus," he
was specifically referring to Christ's humility; but we
can apply this command to *all* of Christ's character
traits. As his followers, we should cultivate the same
gentleness that characterized his life.

Treating others gently

A profile of gentleness as it should appear in our lives
will first include actively seeking to make others feel at
ease, or "restful," in our presence. We should not be
so strongly opinionated or dogmatic that others are
afraid to express their opinions in our presence. Instead, we should be sensitive to others' opinions and
ideas. We should also avoid displaying our commitment to Christian discipleship in such a way as to
make others feel guilty, taking care not to break the
bruised reed of the hurting Christian or snuff out the

smoldering wick of the immature Christian.

Second, gentleness will demonstrate respect for the personal dignity of the other person. Where necessary, it will seek to change a wrong opinion or attitude by persuasion and kindness, not by domination or intimidation. It will studiously avoid coercion by threatening, either directly or indirectly (as Paul, for example, avoided it in his appeal to the Corinthians).

Gentleness will also avoid blunt speech and an abrupt manner, instead seeking to answer everyone with sensitivity and respect, ready to show consideration toward all. The gentle Christian does not feel he has the liberty to "say what I think and let the chips fall where they may." Instead he is sensitive to the reactions of others to his words, and considerate of how others may feel about what he says. When he finds it necessary to wound with his words, he also seeks to bind up those wounds with words of consolation and encouragement.

The gentle Christian will not feel threatened by opposition or resent those who oppose him. Instead, he will seek to gently instruct, looking to God to dissolve the opposition, just as Paul taught Timothy to do in chapter two of his second letter.

Finally, the gentle Christian will not degrade or belittle or gossip about the brother who falls into some sin. Instead he will grieve for him and pray for his repentance. If it is appropriate for him to become personally involved with the erring brother, he will seek to restore him gently, as Paul instructs us in Galatians 6, aware that he himself is also subject to temptation.

The Christian who truly seeks to obey God through gentle character will actively pursue gentleness, striving to clothe himself with it (see Colossians 3:12 and 1 Timothy 6:11). He will place this godly virtue high on his list of spiritual traits and look to God the Holy Spirit to produce this fruit in his life.

Treating others considerately

There is a trait closely related to gentleness that should also characterize the godly Christian who is seeking to manifest the fruit of the Spirit in his life. I have chosen to call it *considerateness*, although according to the commentators, the scriptural term requires several English words to bring out the fullness of its meaning. It appears in Philippians 4:5: "Let your *gentleness* be evident to all." In the *New International Version* it is always translated as *gentleness* or *considerateness* (see Philippians 4:5, 1 Timothy 3:3, Titus 3:2, and James 3:17). The *New American Standard Bible* also uses *gentleness* or *considerateness*, except in Philippians 4:5, where it uses the term *forbearing spirit*.

William Hendriksen says a number of synonyms are necessary to show the broad meaning of this word: yieldedness, reasonableness, big-heartedness, geniality, considerateness.[4] James Adamson uses the word *humane* in his commentary on James and says it describes "the man who is fair, considerate and generous rather than rigid and exacting in his relations with others. . . . It is contrasted with 'strict justice' and is used of judges who do not press the letter of the law. . . . It is also used of people who listen to reason."[5] W. E. Vine says it is "the trait that enables us to look humanely and reasonably at the facts of a case . . . not insisting on the letter of the law.''[6]

The Pharisees, rigid in their absolute adherence to tradition, perfectly demonstrated the opposite of considerateness. They were always asking, "Is it lawful?" They never asked, "Is it kind or reasonable?" Jesus was always getting into trouble with the Pharisees because he constantly broke away from their rigid traditions and, in many cases, exposed their utter absurdity.

The considerate Christian listens to reason and is fair-minded and humane. Instead of insisting on the letter of the law, he asks, "What is the right thing to do in this situation?" This kind of thinking should not be confused, however, with the humanistic philosophy that says, "If it feels right, do it." That philosophy is entirely self-centered and focuses on one's carnal desires. Considerateness, on the other hand, focuses on the other individual and asks, "What is best for him?"

Paul's admonition in Philippians 4:5 provides the proper motivation for a considerate attitude. "Let your gentleness (or considerateness) be evident to all. The Lord is near." We might rephrase it, "The Lord is standing at my shoulder, waiting to see how I will handle the various relationships I have with people today. Will I be rigid and exacting in my demands of them? Or will I be gentle and considerate, seeking to understand the pressures and insecurities they face and making allowances accordingly?" We are to show consideration to all—the store clerk, the bus driver, family members, non-Christians as well as Christians.

I fear that all too often we Christians may be less

humane and considerate than non-believers. We think we are standing on principle when in reality we may be only insisting on our opinion. How do others see us? Do we appear to be rigid, unyielding, and inflexible, or do we come across as genial, reasonable, and humane in our relationships with other people? The Pharisees of Jesus' day had encrusted God's commands with their own traditions. Let us be careful to avoid doing the same thing.

The trait of considerateness is one of the characteristics of heavenly wisdom (see James 3:17). If we want to be wise in God's eyes, we must cultivate this trait of reasonableness and geniality.

Seeking a gentle spirit

I suspect that of all the character traits of godliness in this study, gentleness will be the least appealing to many male readers. For some reason we seem to have difficulty believing that manliness and gentleness can be part of the same personality. Men often want to see gentleness in their mothers and wives, but not in themselves. The macho image of the non-Christian male world has a tendency to rub off, even on us. But the apostle Paul uses the example of a mother's gentleness to describe his own character. He was able to say to the Thessalonian believers, "We were gentle among you, like a mother caring for her little children." A friend of mine, an ex-Marine, often signs his letters, "Keep tough and tender"—tough on ourselves and tender with others. That is the spirit of gentleness.

What are some steps we can take to develop a gentle spirit? First we must decide that this is a trait we really do want to develop. We have to decide that we want to be mild and sensitive in our dealings with others, that we are willing to live without a rigid structure of black-and-white rules. We have to decide if we really want to *care* about people.

Second, we can ask those who know us best and will be honest how we come across to other people. Are we dogmatic and opinionated, blunt and abrupt? Do we seek to intimidate or dominate others by the sheer force of our personality? Do people feel ill at ease in our presence because they think we are silently judging their weaknesses and correcting their faults? If any of these traits are characteristic of us, we must face them honestly and humbly.

As we face our overall need, we should also ask the Holy Spirit to make us aware of specific situations in which we fail to act with gentleness or considerateness. It is not enough to concede in a vague sort of way that we may be lacking in this godly virtue. We need to identify specific instances in which we fall short. Only then will we be driven to pray fervently for the grace of gentleness. And, as always, we ought to memorize one or more passages of Scripture on this topic. I suggest you quickly scan back over this chapter and select at least one Scripture reference to memorize for future meditation. Then put this need on your private prayer list, and pray that God will so work in your life that by his power you will demonstrate the fruit of gentleness.

Notes
1. Bethune, *The Fruit of the Spirit*, page 100.
2. Billy Graham, *The Holy Spirit* (Waco, Texas: Word

Books, 1978), pages 205-206.
3. William Hendriksen, *The Gospel of Matthew* (Grand Rapids, Mich.: Baker Book House, 1973), page 504.
4. William Hendriksen, *Exposition of Philippians* (Grand Rapids, Mich.: Baker Book House, 1962), page 193.
5. James Adamson, "The Epistle of James," *The New International Commentary on the New Testament* (Grand Rapids, Mich.: Eerdmans, 1976), page 155.
6. W. E. Vine, *An Expository Dictionary of New Testament Words*, page 474.

16
Kindness and Goodness

THEREFORE, AS WE HAVE
OPPORTUNITY, LET US DO GOOD
TO ALL PEOPLE, ESPECIALLY TO
THOSE WHO BELONG TO THE
FAMILY OF BELIEVERS.

Galatians 6:10

Kindness and goodness are so closely related that they are often used interchangeably. These two traits finish a natural progression in godly character: patience denotes a godly response to ill-treatment; gentleness defines a godly demeanor toward people at all times; kindness and goodness involve an active desire to recognize and meet the needs of others.

Kindness is a sincere desire for the happiness of others; goodness is the activity calculated to advance that happiness. Kindness is the inner disposition, created by the Holy Spirit, that causes us to be sensitive to the needs of others, whether physical, emotional, or spiritual. Goodness is kindness in action—words and deeds. Because of this close relationship, we often use the two words interchangeably.

231

I tend to think of kindness in terms of our awareness of those around us and the thoughtfulness that we can express to them, almost incidentally. Kindness may be as simple as a smile to a store clerk, a thank-you to a waitress, an encouraging word to an elderly person, or a word of recognition to a small child. None of these expressions is costly in time or money. But they do require a sincere interest in the happiness of those around us. Apart from God's grace, most of us naturally tend to be concerned about *our* responsibilities, *our* problems, *our* plans. But the person who has grown in the grace of kindness has expanded his thinking outside of himself and his interests and has developed a genuine interest in the happiness and well-being of those around him.

Goodness, on the other hand, involves deliberate deeds that are helpful to others. Although the Bible uses the word *good* to refer to what is upright, honorable, and noble about our ethical or moral character, it also uses it to describe actions that are not only good in themselves, but beneficial to others.

Bethune well observes, "The best practical definition of goodness is given in the life and character of Jesus Christ: 'Jesus of Nazareth, who went about doing good.' [Acts 10:38] So far as we resemble Jesus, in his devotion to the welfare of men, do we possess the grace of goodness."[1] Do we aspire to be Christlike? Then we must be continually sensitive to how we might meet the needs of those around us.

God's unfailing kindness

We need to constantly keep in mind that our goal in practicing godliness is to grow in both our devotion to

God and our likeness to him in character and conduct. The New Testament has much to say about the kindness of God. The first mention is in Luke 6: Jesus says that God "is kind to the ungrateful and wicked." Next we find that God's kindness leads sinners toward repentance (Romans 2:4). In Ephesians 2:7, in the context of our utter lostness and sin, Paul speaks of the incomparable riches of God's grace, expressed in his kindness to us in Christ Jesus. He draws a similar contrast in Titus 3: after describing our lost condition, he declares, "But when the kindness and love of God our Savior appeared, he saved us. . . ." It seems the Bible goes out of its way to portray the kindness of God in stark contrast to man's total undeservedness.

What lesson can we draw from these accounts of the kindness of God? He is kind to all men—the ungrateful, the wicked, the utterly lost and hopeless, the rebellious—without distinction. If we are to become Godlike, we, too, must be kind to all men.

Our natural inclination is to show kindness only to those for whom we have some natural affinity—family, friends, likable neighbors. But God shows kindness to those who are most despicable—the ungrateful and wicked. Have you ever tried to be kind to someone who was ungrateful? Unless God's grace was working in your heart in a significant way, your reaction to his ingratitude may well have been, "I'll never do anything for him again!" But God doesn't turn his back on the ungrateful. And so Jesus says to us, "But love your enemies, do good to them, and lend to them without expecting to get anything back" (Luke 6:35).

We need to develop a kind disposition, to be sensitive to others and truly desire their happiness. But sensitivity alone is not enough: the grace of goodness impels us to take action to meet those needs.

Created to do good

Most of us are familiar with Ephesians 2:8-9, which teaches that salvation is by grace, through faith, and not by works. But we should be just as familiar with the next verse: "For we are God's workmanship, created in Christ Jesus to do good works, which God prepared in advance for us to do." This is an amazing statement. Not only are we created in Christ Jesus—born anew for the purpose of doing good works—but we are created to do good works that God *prepared in advance for us to do*. Before we came to know Christ, and, according to Psalm 139:16, before we were even born, God prepared certain good works for us to do.

The *New American Standard Bible* provides a more literal translation of verse 10: "For we are His workmanship, created in Christ Jesus for good works, which God prepared beforehand, that we should walk in them." The word *walk* suggests our common, everyday experience, not the unusual and heroic. We all have a tendency to rise to the special occasions of our lives, but God has created us to do our good works in the midst of the humdrum of daily living. Bethune quotes an earlier writer as saying, "much of the happiness of the world depends upon what are termed little things; and it is rare that God honors us with heroic and famous distinctions in doing good."[2]

Paul aptly illustrates the ordinariness of most good deeds in 1 Timothy 5:9-10. He says that in order for a widow to qualify for church assistance, she must be "well known for her *good deeds*, such as bringing up children, showing hospitality, washing the feet of the saints, helping those in trouble and devoting herself to all kinds of *good deeds*." None of these items on Paul's list is especially exciting or glamorous. They are simply opportunities to do good in the course of daily living. Although this particular passage applies specifically to women, the principle applies equally to men. Most of our opportunities for good deeds will arise out of the course of our daily lives. The challenge to us is to be alert for these opportunities and to see them not as interruptions or inconveniences, but as occasions for doing the good works God has planned for us.

Doing good at work

Perhaps one of the most obvious areas in which God has prepared good works for us to do is our life's calling or vocation. The good works God has prepared for us individually are consistent with the abilities he has given us and the circumstances in which he has placed us. When there is something wrong with my car, and a qualified mechanic fixes it, that is a good deed, in my thinking. If he did it as a part of his calling before God and as a service to his fellowman, it is also a good deed in God's sight, even though he was paid for his work.

Most honorable vocations exist to meet the needs of people. God has ordained his world so that people with various abilities meet various needs. We should think of our vocation, therefore, not as a necessary evil to pay the bills, nor even as an opportunity to become rich, but as the primary path of our Christian walk wherein God has planned good deeds for us to do. Most of us spend half or more of our waking hours at our vocations. If we fail to find opportunities to do good works there, we are throwing away half of our lives as far as fulfilling God's purpose for us here on earth. If we feel our particular job does not allow us to genuinely meet the needs of people, we ought to prayerfully consider a change.

But let me be very clear at this point. I am talking about meeting the *ordinary* needs of people—for clothing, transportation, education, health care, and so on. I am not talking about changing jobs to go into so-called full-time Christian work. If God has called you to that, wonderful! But that is not the only arena of life in which God prepares good works for us.

Evaluate your work situation; if you are a student, consider the work you are thinking of pursuing. Does it lend itself to doing the good deeds God has planned for you? What about your attitude toward your job? Do you view the job as an opportunity to do many of the good deeds God has planned for you by meeting the needs of people, or do you view it as a necessary evil to earn the money you need? If we are to grow in the grace of goodness we must have the right attitude about our vocation.

Many women, of course, do not work outside the home and may wonder how this section on vocation applies to them. For those of you in this situation, homemaking is your vocation, and a rich arena in which to do those good deeds God has called you to do. Few things are more difficult than making a home and rearing children. The dishes, the diapers the washing, the waxing, the cooking and cleaning may at times seem insignificant and distasteful; yet few, if any, vocations render greater benefits to those they serve than godly homemaking. You also may have greater opportunity for good deeds outside the home, such as ministering to the sick and lonely, providing hospitality, preparing meals for others, or caring for someone else's children. Review 1 Timothy 5:10 to see how Paul expected homemakers to be involved in good deeds beyond their own families.

Doing good at home

In Galatians 6:10, Paul tells us to "do good to all people, especially to those who belong to the family of believers." Our good deeds are to be scattered upon all men, Christian and non-Christian. We are to follow the example of our heavenly Father, who "causes his sun to rise on the evil and the good, and sends rain on the righteous and the unrighteous" (Matthew 5:45).

Nevertheless, there is in Paul's instruction a priority of responsibility: first believers, then nonbelievers. I believe we can infer from this order a similar priority involving our families. We are to do good to all men, especially members of our own families. Paul told Timothy, "If anyone does not provide for his relatives, and especially for his immediate family, he has denied the faith and is worse than an unbeliever" (1 Timothy 5:8). Good deeds should begin at home. If we are out doing good deeds for others while neglecting the needs of our spouse, our parents, or our children, we are not practicing the grace of goodness.

I recently heard of a course on biblical marriage in which one of the lessons is entitled, "Who Takes Out the Garbage?" That may be a humorous title to grab our attention, but the author is on to something. Mundane household duties are sore points in many homes, even Christian homes. But for the Christian growing in the grace of goodness, the distasteful and despised duties of the home provide him with the opportunity of doing good deeds for those he loves most.

One of the rich heritages of The Navigators, the organization I work for, is the emphasis on serving others which our founder Dawson Trotman built into the very fabric of the work from its earliest days. As a result, Navigator discipleship training always includes serving others. But when I have had opportunity to address young people on this subject, I encourage them to begin at home. It is a lot easier to clean up after a weekend conference than to clean out Dad's garage back home. Somehow it seems more spiritual to baby-sit some other lady's children for free than to help Mom with the dishes after Sunday dinner.

Husbands, most of us have a lot of growing to do in this area of good deeds at home. There are a lot of little things we can do *in* the house, as well as *around* it, to be more sensitive in meeting our wives' needs. Who *does* take out the garbage at your house? The best teaching is by example. If we would train our children to do good deeds (and they *must* be trained —they do not learn it naturally), then we must be examples to them. I wonder how many boys growing up in Christian homes ever have the privilege of seeing their Dad do the dishes or mop the kitchen floor? Let us do good to all, but especially to our own family.

Doing good to all people

Good deeds in our vocations and in our homes are important, but there is still a big world out there for each of us, with numerous opportunities for doing good. Thus far I have emphasized meeting the physical needs of people; but being a disposition to promote the happiness of others, goodness certainly directs much of its energies to the spiritual and eternal needs of others. Here again, God has prepared good works for each of us, consistent with our gifts and circumstances. We need to pray, "Lord, what will you have me to do?" and then we should *do* it.

Although we do need to observe Paul's priority in Galatians 6 for "the family of believers," let us not overlook the "all people" referred to in the same verse. Because opportunities for doing good are virtually unlimited, we must be sensitive to God's Holy Spirit as he selects opportunities for us.

One kind of behavior we must guard against is the impulsive and often superficial response to the needs of others. On this point Bethune very wisely remarks,

> True goodness is not merely impulsive, but rational and considerate—It will therefore pause, and be at some trouble to inquire what service, and how best may it be rendered. . . . Goodness should be willing to give time, and thought, and patience, and even labor; not mere money and kind word. and compassionate looks.[3]

True goodness is self-sacrificing, not only of money but of time. Like the Macedonian Christians who gave "even beyond their ability" (2 Corinthians 8:3), the Christian who wants to do good for others will often have to give time he does not have. Often this is an act of faith just as much as giving money we think we cannot afford. We will always be too busy to help others, unless we truly grasp the importance God puts on our doing good deeds for others.

One of the less obvious but more critical needs that many (shall I say most?) people have is for someone to listen to them. They don't need our advice as much as our attention. A friend of mine went through a personal tragedy. I couldn't think of anything to say, so I hesitated to contact him. Finally I called and invited him to lunch. For an hour I sat and listened—no advice, just listened. The only time I talked was to draw him out. One thing he said stuck in my mind: "It really meant a lot to me when you called last night." We hadn't even gotten together yet. Just the phone call and the invitation to lunch encouraged him; just realizing that someone cared meant a lot to him.

I believe most people, Christians as well as non-Christians, are so starved for the genuine interest of one other person that a little bit of concern from someone who cares goes a mighty long way. One of the most plaintive statements in the Bible is David's cry in Psalm 142:4, "No one cares for my soul" (NASB). Do you know someone who possibly feels that way? If so, you have an opportunity to do good to that person by saying, "I just want you to know I care."

True goodness is not only self-sacrificing, it is also untiring. It does not "become weary in doing good" (Galatians 6:9). It is one thing to do good in a few, or even in a number of, isolated instances; it is quite another to face cheerfully the prospect of doing some particular deed of goodness day in and day out for an interminable period of time, particularly if those deeds are taken for granted by the recipients. But true goodness does not look to the recipients, nor even to the results, of its deeds for its reward. It looks to God alone, and, finding his smile of approval, it gains the needed strength to carry on.

Perhaps one of the most sobering statements in the Bible is found in Hebrews 12:14: "without holiness no one will see the Lord." It is not my profession, but my holiness that proves the validity of my Christian experience and my possession of eternal life. But Jesus' account of the judgment day recorded in Matthew 25 is just as sobering. There the test is good deeds: feeding the hungry, giving water to the thirsty, clothing the needy, showing hospitality to the stranger, attending to the sick, and visiting those in prison. Jesus is teaching in that passage not that doing good deeds earns our admittance to heaven, but that they are necessary and vital evidences that we are bound for heaven. Bethune explains,

> And so in the judgment day, the inquiry will be made not into our opinions or professions alone, but into our deeds, as proving the correctness of our faith and the sincerity of our professions. Never can we know that we are in the right way, except we walk in the footsteps of Him, who did good in all

his life and death. He came from heaven to do good on earth, that we in doing good might tread the path to heaven.[4]

Without holiness no one will see the Lord. The essence of Matthew 25:31-46 is that without goodness no one will see the Lord. Both of these thoughts are very sobering to the one who takes seriously the words of Scripture.

Watching for opportunities

One objective in studying godly character traits is to become more conscious of the vital importance of some of the perhaps lesser-known qualities. Have you ever reflected, for example, upon how important good deeds are to Jesus, as he indicates in Matthew 25:31-46? What better stimulation to good deeds can we have than to meditate on that passage of Scripture from time to time? Or you might prayerfully consider the truth of Ephesians 2:10, asking God to make clear to you some of the good works that he has prepared for you to do.

Consider your gifts, your talents, your vocation, and your circumstances as a special trust from God with which to serve him by serving others. As Peter says, "Each one should use whatever gift he has received to serve others, faithfully administering God's grace in its various forms" (1 Peter 4:10). Remember that you are responsible not for doing all the good that needs to be done in the world, but for doing what God has planned for you.

Remember also that most opportunities for doing good come across the ordinary path of our day.

Don't look for the spectacular; few people ever have the opportunity to pull a victim from the wreckage of a flaming automobile. *All* of us have the opportunity to administer the kind or encouraging word, to do the little, perhaps unseen, deed that makes life more pleasant for someone else.

Accept the cost of good deeds in time, thought, and effort. But remember that opportunities for doing good are not interruptions in God's plan for us, but part of that plan. We always have time to do what God wants us to do.

Acknowledge your need of his divine grace to enlarge your soul and enable you to look beyond yourself to the concerns and needs of those around you. Then come to his throne with confidence to receive the grace you need to grow in the fruit of kindness and goodness. May it be said of each of us as it was of Dorcas, that we are "always doing good and helping the poor" (Acts 9:36).

Notes

1. Bethune, *The Fruit of the Spirit*, page 117.
2. Bethune, page 126.
3. Bethune, pages 127-128.
4. Bethune, page 132.

17
Love

*. . AND OVER ALL THESE VIRTUES
PUT ON LOVE, WHICH BINDS THEM
ALL TOGETHER IN PERFECT UNITY.*

Colossians 3:14

When Paul lists those godly traits he calls the fruit of
the Spirit, he puts love first—very likely to emphasize
its importance. Love is the overall grace from which all
the others grow; I have reserved it for last in these
studies, because, as Paul indicates in Colossians 3:14,
love binds all the other virtues together in perfect unity.

Devotion to God is the only motivation acceptable to God for the development and exercise of
Christian character (see chapter five). But devotion to
God finds its outward expression in loving one another. Or, to state it another way, our devotion to
God is validated by our love for other people. As the
apostle John puts it, "For anyone who does not love
his brother, whom he has seen, cannot love God,
whom he has not seen. And he has given us this

245

command. Whoever loves God must also love his brother" (1 John 4:20-21).

We cannot truly love God without loving one another. To recognize that there is someone I do not love is to say to God, "I do not love you enough to love that person." This is not to deny the reality of spiritual struggle in loving a particular person, because it often exists. I am referring to the attitude of not even wanting to love the person, of being content to allow a lack of love for someone to reside in my heart unchecked and unchallenged.

Jesus linked loving God to loving man in Matthew 22:37-40, when he was asked about the greatest commandment in the Law. George Bethune observes of this passage, "The command to man to 'love God with all his heart, and with all his mind, and with all his strength,' is followed by a command to 'love his neighbor as himself,' which could not be, unless love to our neighbor is included in love to God; for how else can we give all our heart to God, and love ourselves and our neighbor too?"[1]

Devotion to God is the ultimate motivation for Christian character, but it is also true that love for our brother is the more proximate motivation for the exercise of Christian graces among one another. If we rephrased the virtues of love in 1 Corinthians 13 in terms of motivational statements, they might sound something like this:

● I am patient with you because I love you and want to forgive you.

● I am kind to you because I love you and want to help you.

● I do not envy your possessions or your gifts

because I love you and want you to have the best.

• I do not boast about my attainments because I love you and want to hear about yours.

• I am not proud because I love you and want to esteem you before myself.

• I am not rude because I love you and care about your feelings.

• I am not self-seeking because I love you and want to meet your needs.

• I am not easily angered by you because I love you and want to overlook your offenses.

• I do not keep a record of your wrongs because I love you, and "love covers a multitude of sins."

Expressing love in this manner, as a motivational factor, helps us see what Paul had in mind when he said that love binds together all the virtues of Christian character. Love is not so much a character trait as the inner disposition of the soul that produces them all. Bethune says love is "a holy, abiding and vigorous spirit, which rules the whole man, ever directing him to the humble and loving fulfillment of all his duties to God and man."[2] But although love may be more a motivational force than an actual display of Christian virtue, it *always* results in actions on our part. Love inclines us and directs us to be kind, to forgive, to give of ourselves to one another. Therefore, Peter says to us, "Above all, love each other deeply" (1 Peter 4:8).

God is love

We have already noted in chapter ten that the apostle John makes two statements concerning the essential nature of God: "God is light" and "God is love." Love is not defined here as an action, nor even as a character trait, but as an essential part of God's nature. As Bethune notes, "God was love long before he had made any creatures to be the objects of his love, even from all eternity."[3]

God is infinitely glorious in all his attributes, but the Bible seems to give preeminence to his holiness and to his goodness or love. In Exodus 33 there is an instructive relationship between God's goodness and God's glory. In response to Moses' request, "Now show me your glory," God replies, "I will cause all my goodness to pass in front of you, and I will proclaim my name, the Lord, in your presence" (verses 18-19). Yet in verse 22 God says, "When my glory passes by. . . ." It appears from the correlation of verses 18 and 22 that God equates his glory with his goodness. And how does God describe his goodness? Exodus 34:6-7 says, "And he passed in front of Moses, proclaiming, 'The Lord, the Lord, the compassionate and gracious God, slow to anger, abounding in love and faithfulness, maintaining love to thousands, and forgiving wickedness, rebellion and sin.'"

The children of Israel seemed to recognize God's goodness as the expression of his glory. At the dedication of Solomon's temple, according to 2 Chronicles 7:2, the glory of the Lord so filled the temple that the priests could not enter. Then verse 3 tells us,

> When all the Israelites saw the fire coming down and the glory of the Lord above the temple, they knelt on the pavement with their faces to the ground, and they worshiped and gave thanks to the Lord, saying, "He is good; his love endures forever."

Notice the Israelites' response when they saw God's glory: "He is good." God's goodness is the preeminent expression of his glory. If we desire to be Godlike and to glorify God in our lives, therefore, we must make the cultivation and exercise of love in our hearts an urgent priority. There are three overall prayer requests I make for myself and for others for whom I pray: that I and they would grow in holiness, humility, and love. Of these three, however, love has priority, for if I love God I will seek to be holy, and if I love other people I will seek to be humble, putting their interests ahead of mine.

If love to God and to our neighbor should be our highest priority, then it is important for us to know how love expresses itself. First Corinthians 13 is, of course, the most familiar description of love. And the list of qualities covered in that passage have, for the most part, already been addressed in previous chapters of this book. There are two other Scripture passages, however, that seem to sum up the essence of love into two overall traits that will be easily remembered. These passages are 1 John 3:16-18 and 4:7-11.

Love gives, whatever the cost

In 1 John 3:16 John says, "This is how we know what love is: Jesus Christ laid down his life for us." The key idea here is that *love gives, even at great cost to itself*. Jesus gave his life for us. John 3:16 tells us that the Father so loved that he gave his only Son to die for us. In Jesus' incarnation and death, both the Father and the Son gave in response to our desperate plight. Nothing but the Savior's incarnation and death would suffice to rescue us. The cost was infinite, but God the Father and God the Son loved us so much they did not hesitate to pay the cost to meet our need.

John says in his epistle that we too should give even at great cost to ourselves: We should "lay down our lives for our brothers." In the context of Jesus' sacrifice, John's challenge to us seems overwhelming and impossible—the ultimate act of love. But John's application is very practical and down-to-earth: He asks that we share with our brother in need. We are to do this out of pity and compassion, however, not duty. We are to put our love into practice by meeting our brother's need—even at great cost to us.

There are tremendous needs in the world today, and we Christians ought to be involved in meeting those needs. John is very clear on this point: "If anyone has material possessions and sees his brother in need but has no pity on him, how can the love of God be in him?" Paul tells us the Macedonian Christians exhibited this kind of love: "Out of the most severe trial, their overflowing joy and their extreme poverty welled up in rich generosity. For I testify that they gave as much as they were able, and even beyond their ability" (2 Corinthians 8:2-3). They gave out of love and at great cost to themselves to meet the material needs of Christian brothers in Jerusalem, whom they had never even met. We should give to our church and to the work of missions, but we should not overlook the fact that the most well-known passage in the Bible on giving, 2 Corinthians 8—9, has to do with giving to the poor.

But material needs are not the only ones our brother has. Often he needs a listening ear, a word of encouragement, or a helping hand. But to meet those needs requires us to give of ourselves—our time, our attention, and often our heart. This can be more difficult than giving money. Paul said of Timothy, "I have no one else like him, who takes a genuine interest in your welfare" (Philippians 2:20). As he compliments Timothy, Paul adds a striking indictment of others: "For everyone looks out for his own interests, not those of Jesus Christ" (verse 21).

To meet the non-material needs of others costs getting out of ourselves, our concerns, and our interests. We cannot take a genuine interest in the welfare of others, as did Timothy, unless we are willing to become involved in their interests and their concerns. And we cannot do this unless we are willing to forego our own interests. But love willingly pays the price.

Love sacrifices to forgive

The second passage in which John instructs us in the meaning of love is 1 John 4:7-11. Immediately following his declaration that "God is love," John says,

> This is how God showed his love among us: He sent his one and only Son into the world that we might live through him. This is love: not that we loved God, but that he loved us and sent his Son as an atoning sacrifice for our sins. Dear friends, since God so loved us, we also ought to love one another.

Once again John points us to God's sacrifice in sending his Son into the world that we might live through him. But the central thought is that *God gave in order that he might forgive*. He sent his Son as an atoning sacrifice for our sins. The concept of atonement is best expressed by the marginal reading of the *New International Version*: ''the one who would turn aside his wrath, taking away'' our sins. God gave his Son, who took away our sins by bearing in his own body God's wrath, thus turning away that wrath from us. God's justice required that our sin be punished, and forgiveness was impossible as long as justice was unsatisfied. So God gave his Son in order that he might forgive us. He forgave at great cost to himself.

Now John once again applies God's love to our relationships with one another. He says since God so loved us, we also ought to love one another. Do we love one another enough to forgive each other, with or without apologies for wrongs done to us? So often we want to exact the last ounce of remorse and repentance from our erring brother before we will even consider forgiving him. But God did not do this. When we were still sinners, still his enemies, he sent his Son to die for us so that he might forgive us. And John urges us to do likewise.

Forgiveness cost God his Son on the cross, but what does it cost us to forgive one another? Forgiving costs us our sense of justice. We all have this innate sense deep within our souls, but it has been perverted by our selfish sinful natures. We want to see ''justice'' done, but the justice we envision satisfies our own interests. We must realize that justice *has* been done. God is the only rightful administrator of justice in all of creation, and his justice has been satisfied. In order to forgive our brother, we must be satisfied with God's justice and forego the satisfaction of our own.

I recall a personal struggle a number of years ago to love one of my brothers in Christ. One evening the Holy Spirit addressed to my mind the rather startling question, "Do you believe I love him just as he is?" I hadn't thought of that before, but I did concede that surely God must love him just as he was, faults and all. And then God pressed this question to my mind, "If I can love him, can you?" God was teaching me to love as he loves, to forgive as he forgives. And love forgives at great cost to itself; it does not demand justice or even changed behavior from its brother.

This forgiving aspect of love enables us to be patient with one another and to live at peace with one another. It enables us to deal gently with our brother, even when he sins against us. If we are to grow in the grace of love, we must be ready to forgive, even at great cost to ourselves.

Love reaches out

Often in our teaching on love, we stress—and rightly so—that biblical love is not emotions or feelings, but attitudes and actions that seek the best interests of the other person, regardless of how we feel toward him. Vine says, for example, "Christian love . . . is not an impulse from the feelings, it does not always run with the natural inclinations, nor does it spend itself only upon those for whom some affinity is discovered."[4] An illustration from *The Pursuit of Holiness* provides an example of this kind of love:

> Suppose you were meditating on 1 Corinthians 13, the great love chapter. As you think about the chapter, you realize the importance of love and you also

see the practical outworkings of love: Love is patient and kind and does not envy. You ask yourself, "Am I impatient or unkind or envious toward anyone?" As you think about this, you realize you are envious toward Joe at work who seems to be getting all the breaks. You confess this sin to God, being very specific to name Joe and your sinful reaction to his good fortune. You ask God to bless him even more and to give you a spirit of contentment so that you will not continue to envy Joe, but will instead love him. You might memorize 1 Corinthians 13:4 and think about it as you see Joe at work. You even look for ways to help him. Then you do the same thing tomorrow and the next day and the next till finally you see God working a spirit of love in your heart toward Joe.[5]

So love is very much a matter of actions rather than emotions. However, although this emphasis on *acts of love* is certainly necessary, we can sometimes give the impression that love doesn't involve any emotion—that it is entirely an act of the will, of one's duty, regardless of how one feels. We can even promote the "I can love him but I can't like him" type of attitude. The Bible does not support such an unbalanced concept of love.

In describing the Christian's love toward his brother, the Bible uses such expressions as "love one another deeply, from the heart" (1 Peter 1:22) and "Be devoted to one another in brotherly love" (Romans 12:10). Other translations choose such words as *fervently, fondly,* and *affectionately* in the same passages to describe the love Christians ought to have for one another. Three different writers use the expression "brotherly love" or "love as brothers," all indicating that Christian love is to be characterized by an affection that family members have—or ought to have—for one another (see Hebrews 13:1 and 1 Peter 3:8).

All of these passages from the Bible indicate that our emotions are involved. We are to reach out and embrace our brother with a deep fervency of spirit, in our hearts if not in actuality. Obviously such a fervency of spirit cannot substitute for loving actions, but surely it should accompany them. We dare not settle for less.

From the contents of Paul's epistles to the churches, we can safely say the two churches that caused him the most grief were Corinth and Galatia. Yet listen to the emotion in Paul's voice when he writes to the Corinthians, "For I wrote you out of great distress and anguish of heart and with many tears, not to grieve you but to let you know the depth of my love for you" (2 Corinthians 2:4). And to the Galatians he wrote, "My dear children, for whom I am again in the pains of childbirth until Christ is formed in you, how I wish I could be with you now and change my tone, because I am perplexed about you!" (4:19-20). Distress, anguish, tears, and pains of childbirth are all terms calculated to express the deep emotion of Paul's love toward these people. That their actions made them difficult to love only deepened the intensity of his love for them. And that love was not just an impersonal act of writing them letters of correction in their best interest; he reached out and embraced them even while he rebuked them.

One of the greatest moments of my Christian life occurred one day when I opened my arms and warmly embraced a brother in Christ whom I had somewhat disliked for several years. God had so dealt with me that I finally realized that to think about anyone, "I will love him, but I can't like him" was a great deal less than God's standard of love and was therefore a sinful attitude on my part.

Love is more than a mere act of the will. Going back again to Bethune's definition, love is a *vigorous* spirit that rules the whole man, ever directing him to the humble and loving fulfillment of his duties to God and man. We should do more than just *decide* to do acts of love: we should *desire* to do them. This is not to say we are to do acts of love only when we feel like doing them; it is to say we are not to content ourselves merely with acts of the will, good as those acts may be. We are to lay hold on God in prayer until he gives us that vigorous and loving spirit that delights to reach out and embrace our brother and to meet his need or forgive his sin, even if it is at great cost to ourselves.

Growing in love

It is obvious that the love we have been considering can be produced in our hearts only by the Spirit of God. Paul wrote to the Thessalonian believers, "You yourselves have been taught by God to love each other" (1 Thessalonians 4:9). And yet just a few words later Paul says, "Yet we urge you, brothers, to [love] more and more" (verse 10). Once again, and especially as we draw to the close of these studies on godly character, we must review this principle: Godlike character is both the fruit of the Spirit as he works within us and the result of our personal efforts. We are both totally dependent upon his working within us and totally responsible for our own character development. This is an apparent contradiction to our either-or type of thinking, but it is a truth taught over and over in the Scriptures.

How then can we fulfill our responsibility to love "more and more"? Recognizing that love is an inner disposition of the soul produced only by the Holy Spirit, what can we do to fulfill our responsibility? First, as we have already seen, the Spirit of God uses his word to transform us. Therefore, if we want to grow in love, we must saturate our minds with Scriptures that describe love and show its importance to us. First Corinthians 13:1-3, for example, tells us of the emptiness of all knowledge, abilities, and zeal apart from love. First Corinthians 13:4-7 describes love in terms of specific attitudes and actions. Romans 13:8-10 describes love in terms of fulfilling the law of God in our lives. We have already looked at the two passages in 1 John in terms of giving and forgiving. Do you truly want to grow in love? Then you must begin by meditating on some of these love passages.

The second thing we must do is pray for the Holy Spirit to apply his word to our hearts and to our daily lives. Paul did not just exhort the Thessalonians to grow in love; he looked to the Lord to work in their hearts: "May the Lord make your love increase and overflow for each other and for everyone else, just as ours does for you" (1 Thessalonians 3:12). As we see instances in our lives of failing to love, we should confess them to God, asking him to help us grow in those specific areas and be more sensitive to such occasions in the future.

Finally, we must obey. We must do those things that love dictates. We must do no harm to our neighbor (Romans 13:10); we must meet our neighbor's needs and forgive our neighbor's wrongs against us. We must put his interests before our own, and we must reach out and embrace our brother in Christ. But we must do all this in dependence upon the Holy Spirit, who works in us to will and to act according to his good purpose.

Does this all sound too methodical? Can we in fact structure love? No; nor can we structure the work of the Holy Spirit in our lives. But we can structure our responsibilities in seeking to grow in love. We can decide to meditate on Scripture—and set aside a time to do it. We can decide to pray over our need to grow in love—and set aside time to do it. We can think of people who need our time, our interest, or our money, and plan to meet those needs. We can admit our failures to love in specific situations and bring those failures to God in confession and dependence upon him for his help in the future.

All these things we can do, and we *must* do, if we are to grow in the grace of love. But we must do them all in the utter realization that only God can cause love to grow within our souls. And we know that it is his will that we grow in love.

As we do our part, we can count on God to perform his, not because our working obligates him to work, but because he is a gracious and loving God, and he wants us to become gracious and loving children of his.

Notes
1. Bethune, *The Fruit of the Spirit*, page 40.
2. Bethune, page 41.
3. Bethune, page 38.
4. W. E. Vine, *An Expository Dictionary of New Testament Words*, page 693.
5. Jerry Bridges, *The Pursuit of Holiness*, pages 104-105.

18
Reaching
the Goal

—

I HAVE FOUGHT THE GOOD FIGHT,
I HAVE FINISHED THE RACE, I
HAVE KEPT THE FAITH.

2 Timothy 4:7

The practice of godliness is a discipline. It requires serious commitment and persevering effort to reach the goal. Writing to the Philippians near the end of his life from a Roman prison cell, Paul acknowledged that he had not yet reached it. He was still running the race of godliness; he still wanted to know Christ more and become more like him.

What kept Paul going as he strained toward what was ahead? What motivating factor did he count on when he wrote to Timothy, ''train yourself to be godly,'' fully knowing that such training was an arduous task, full of difficulties and discouragements? Someone has remarked that desire without discipline breeds disappointment, but discipline without desire breeds drudgery. Was the pursuit of a godly life a drudgery to Paul? Did he expect Timothy in his discipline toward godliness to simply grit his teeth and endure the Christian life?

Paul's motivation

Paul's description of his own practice of godliness, in Philippians 3:12-14, answers these questions. He was deeply motivated. There is no suggestion of either disappointment or drudgery. He was running a disciplined race, but he was running it with strong desire. What was the source of Paul's motivation, the object of his strong desire? Let's take a close look at the passage in Philippians:

> Not that I have already obtained all this, or have already been made perfect, but I press on to take hold of that for which Christ Jesus took hold of me. Brothers, I do not consider myself yet to have taken hold of it. But one thing I do: Forgetting what is behind and straining toward what is ahead, I press on toward the goal to win the prize for which God has called me heavenward in Christ Jesus.

Paul admitted that he had not obtained the goal of godliness. He had not yet been made perfect; he was still running the race. Note the intensity, though, of his running. He declares, "I press on . . . straining toward what is ahead." The word translated "press on" is the same word translated "pursue" in such passages as 1 Timothy 6:11, 2 Timothy 2:22, and 1 Peter 3:11. It is also the same word for "persecute," which means to track down and harass or torment. It is a word of great intensity. "Strain toward" brings to our minds the attitude of the runner with his eye fixed firmly on the goal, his body bent forward, every muscle and nerve in his body straining to reach the goal. Anyone who has ever seen the look of agony on the faces of runners straining for the tape can readily recognize the intensity conveyed by the verb "strain toward." Yet this intensity was Paul's experience, day in and day out. Paul never had an off season; he never slacked off in his efforts. It was a lifelong discipline. How could he sustain such intensity? Was it because of his intense personality, and thus unique to him and those of like temperament? Or was there a motivation in Paul's heart that should be the common experience of every Christian?

In verses 12 and 14, Paul speaks of two motivating factors. In verse 12 he presses on to take hold of that for which Christ Jesus took hold of him. In verse 14 he presses on to win the prize for which God had called him heavenward in Christ Jesus. The first speaks of God's *objective* for him; the second speaks of God's *reward* for him. Let us look at each of these to see how they so strongly motivated Paul.

Christ's objective for us

Paul pressed on to take hold of that for which Christ took hold of him. He earnestly strove to reach Christ's objective for him. What was this objective? Titus 2:14 tells us that Christ "gave himself for us to redeem us from all wickedness and to purify for himself a people that are his very own, eager to do what is good." Christ Jesus' objective in dying for us was to redeem us *from* sin—not merely from its penalty, but from its power and dominion. The same thought is expressed in the word *purify*, which speaks of the inward cleansing from the pollution and defilement of sin.

Ephesians 5:25-27 expresses the same idea of Christ giving himself for his church "to make her holy, cleansing her by the washing with water through the word, and to present her to himself as a radiant church, without stain or wrinkle or any other blemish, but holy and blameless." That is Christ's objective for us. That is why he died. That is the purpose for which he took hold of Paul on the Damascus road and for which he takes hold of us individually to bring us to faith in himself. He died to save us not only from the guilt of sin, but from sin's power and pollution. He died not to make us happy, but to make us holy.

But there is still more to Christ's objective for us. Titus 2:14 also speaks of us as "a people that are his very own, eager to do what is good." A people of "his very own" refers to his Lordship in our lives: "You are not your own; you were bought at a price" (1 Corinthians 6:19-20). "Eager to do what is good" refers to the working out of the fruit of the Spirit, the traits of godly character in our lives.

This, then, is the objective for which Christ Jesus took hold of Paul, and for which he has taken hold of us: He intends to make us holy—to purify us from the pollution of sin in our lives. He intends to be Lord of our lives, and he intends that we exhibit the traits of godly character.

That was Paul's objective also. That was the goal toward which he pressed; the aim of his strenuous effort. It would have been unthinkable to Paul to pursue any other aim in life than that for which Christ Jesus had taken hold of him.

Note how God-centered Paul's motivation was. It was the keen awareness of Christ's objective for him that caused Paul to press on with such intensity. How different we so often are from Paul. All too often we are motivated by desires other than Christ's objectives for us. As I have observed earlier, we may often be motivated by a desire for "victory" or a desire to "feel good about ourselves," or a desire to conform to the lifestyle of the Christian fellowship with which we have become associated. We may even be motivated by pride, by a desire for a good reputation in the community, especially in our church or Christian group.

None of these motivations will sustain a daily "pressing on" such as that which characterized Paul's life and which should characterize ours. Some of them, such as the desire to conform and the desire for reputation, focus on goals that fall far short of Paul's goal of godly perfection. These goals can be easily met; we don't have to deal with inner corruption, only outward acts. Other goals such as a desire for "victory" or "feeling good about ourselves" are basically self-centered goals. Instead of spurring us on, they all too often discourage us because they set up within us a struggle between two self-centered desires: the desire to feel good about ourselves and the desire to indulge ourselves.

The currently popular desire to "feel good about myself" is quite distinct from genuine godly self-respect, however. The former focuses on self; the latter focuses on God. The former depends upon our own efforts or the affirmation of other people; the latter depends upon God's grace. Godly self-respect is possible when we realize that we are created in the image of God, that we are accepted by God solely on the merits of Jesus Christ, that nothing we will ever do will cause him to love us more or love us less, and that he has a plan for our lives and will enable us through his Spirit to live out that plan. The person with godly self-respect freely admits that nothing good lives in his sinful nature. But he also knows that nothing—not even his sin or failures—can separate him from God's love. He has decided that since God has accepted him on the basis of his grace, he will accept himself on the same basis: God's grace. He therefore looks outside of himself to Christ to find his self-respect. He strives toward the goal not to win acceptance, but because he has already been accepted.

The first of Paul's motivating drives, then, was the desire to take hold of that for which Jesus Christ took hold of him. He desired perfection in godly character, though he knew he would never attain it in this life. But he knew it was for this purpose that Jesus died for him, and he longed for that purpose to be fulfilled so Jesus Christ might be satisfied. This same earnest desire should motivate each of us today.

The desire for God's prize

Not only did Paul press on toward Christ's objective for him; he also pressed on to win the prize for which God called him heavenward in Christ Jesus. What is this prize which so motivated Paul that he strove for it with great intensity? Jac J. Müller answers, "the prize of this calling toward which he presses forward with all his might, is the everlasting, heavenly glory."[1] Paul knew his citizenship was in heaven, and he pressed on to obtain that heavenly prize. His mind was not on earthly things, but on the glory that would be his when Christ transformed his lowly body so that it would be like Christ's glorious body.

If the prize, however, is the glory of eternal life, wasn't Paul already assured of that reward? Would a man strive with Paul's intensity to win what was already his as a gift of God's grace? The Bible is quite clear that the glory of eternal life is given to us solely through the redeeming work of Jesus Christ on the cross. It is the gift of God (Romans 6:23); it is by grace through faith—not by works (Ephesians 2:8-9). Yet it is also true that this gift cannot be taken for granted. True grace always produces vigilance rather than complacency; it always produces perseverance rather than indolence. Saving faith always manifests itself by the pursual of the heavenly goal.

The same Savior who said, "I give them eternal life, and they shall never perish" (John 10:28) also said, "Strive to enter by the narrow door; for many, I tell you, will seek to enter and will not be able" (Luke 13:24, NASB). The same apostle Peter who said, "In his great mercy he has given us new birth . . . into an inheritance that can never perish" (1 Peter 1:3-4), also said, "Therefore, my brothers, be all the more eager to make your calling and election sure" (2 Peter 1:10). And Paul himself, who said nothing "will be able to separate us from the love of God that is in Christ Jesus our Lord" (Romans 8:39), also said, "I beat my body and make it my slave so that after I have preached to others, I myself will not be disqualified for the prize" (1 Corinthians 9:27).

Commenting on Paul's strong language to the Corinthians, Charles Hodge says,

> What an argument and reproof is this! The reckless
> and listless Corinthians thought they could safely in-
> dulge themselves to the very verge of sin, while this
> devoted apostle considered himself engaged in a life
> struggle for his salvation. This same apostle, how-
> ever, who evidently acted on the principle that the
> righteous scarcely are saved, and that the kingdom
> of heaven suffereth violence, at other times breaks
> out in the most joyful assurance of salvation. . . .
> The one state of mind is the necessary condition of
> the other.[2]

This is the great antinomy of the New Testament: the
apparent contradiction between grace and personal
responsibility. But it is there, and we avoid it at our
peril.

But Paul was not concerned about theological
knots at this point. He was simply baring his soul
about the deep wellsprings of personal motivation,
the secret of his ceaseless drive toward the goal. And
what is that inner source? It is the glory of heaven.

Over and over again the Bible holds forth the
glory of heaven as a motivation for Christian perseverance (see, for example, Romans 5:1-5, 2 Corinthians
5:1-5, Hebrews 12:22-29, and 1 Peter 4:12-13). One
of the old masters of the Puritan era, Thomas Manton, said of this motivation,

> What is the reason Paul was so earnest that a little
> grace would not content him, but he was striving for
> more so earnestly and zealously? He was called to
> enjoy a high prize, a glorious reward. There is ex-
> cellent glory set before us; this race is not for trifles.

Christians are the more cold and careless in the
spiritual life because they do not oftener think of
heaven.[3]

How do we respond to the motivational drives of
the apostle Paul? Does the love of Christ so compel us
that we also press on to take hold of that goal of godly
perfection for which Christ Jesus took hold of us?
Does the glory of heaven and the prospect of that
prize draw us forward so that we too strain toward
what is ahead? We have considered many of the
character traits of the godly person. Here, though, are
two over-arching traits that clearly distinguish the
godly person. His attention is focused on Christ's objective for him, and his eye is fixed on heaven. He is
God-centered in his devotion, and he strives to be
Godlike in his character.

In Philippians 3:12-14, Paul describes himself as
still running the race. In 2 Timothy 4:7, he speaks as
one who has now finished the race: "I have fought the
good fight, I have finished the race, I have kept the
faith." Dear Reader, when you and I come to the end
of life's journey, will we, too, be able to utter those
words? Only if we have obeyed Paul's command in
1 Timothy 4:7-8 to Timothy and to us: "Train
yourself to be godly," and if we have kept before us
the companion promise, "godliness has value for all
things, holding promise for both the present life and
the life to come."

Notes

1. Müller, "The Epistles of Paul to the Philippians and
   to Philemon," *The New International Commentary*

on the New Testament, page 124.
2. Hodge, *An Exposition of the First Epistle to the Corinthians* (Edinburgh: The Banner of Truth Trust: 1959), page 169.
3. Thomas Manton, *The Complete Works of Thomas Manton*, Vol. 16 (Worthington, Penn.: Maranatha Publications, n.d.), page 178.